From Medic

"At the pinnacle of her career as a well-respected British Genitourinary physician, Dr Anona Blackwell decided that there is more to healing than standard drugs and surgery, and bravely embarked on a journey to discover an alternative toolkit—everything from spiritual healing to medical intuition. *From Medic to Mystic*, which recounts this journey, is nothing less than a blueprint for a new medicine, a wake-up call for every doctor and essential reading for every patient who believes that true healing encompasses the spiritual. Read this book and reclaim your right to true holistic medicine."

— LYNNE McTAGGART, bestselling author of *The Field*, *The Intention Experiment* and *The Power of Eight*

"*From Medic to Mystic* is an enchanting book. It's a work-of-art for the soul and everyone who reads this delightful book will enjoy every page. I loved it."

— CAROLINE MYSS, author of *Anatomy of the Spirit* and *Conversations With the Divine*

"In this bold, compassionate, often funny, and always illuminating book, Dr. Anona Blackwell reveals the importance of addressing the nature of spirit, not only in medicine but in ourselves. This is a brave book that peers under the lid of the scientific box and encourages all of us to speak to a bigger truth. Each of us carries a piece of an incomplete puzzle. It's time to share our unique perspective and explore the larger picture that is revealed. A great read, well done!"

— DR SYNTHIA ANDREWS, ND, author of several books on consciousness and healing including *The Path of Energy* series and *Subtle Energy Work*

"The belief that science and spirituality are mutually exclusive is still widespread. Anona Blackwell's life story is a luminous testimony to the contrary. *From Medic to Mystic* is the compelling autobiography of a Lancet-published physician who has the courage to share her own 'paranormal' experiences, which are rooted in her as firmly—and perhaps as complementarily—as her remarkable medical training and career.

The author tells us with great humour about her unconventional yet fascinating journey, which has been both challenging at times and rewarding in the positive impact it has had on countless patients and others. Anona has a secret, long kept quiet in the competitive academic medical world—not very receptive to spiritual questions—but one that she has finally embraced and explored further with pride and joy. Her secret lies in the connection that she has had since childhood—and that arguably all human beings have without being fully aware of it—with the spiritual dimension ('The sixth sense I had been born with', page 45). Alongside her academic and research work, she has become a registered spiritual healer. When science and spirituality meet, patients greatly benefit. In Anona's words: 'We have access to far greater powers and abilities than we imagine', page 48.

I highly recommend this brilliant book, which convincingly shows that science and spirituality are not antinomic but can complement each other for the greater good of patients."

— EVELYN ELSAESSER, After-Death Communications (ADCs) and Near-Death Experiences (NDEs) expert, author of *Spontaneous Contacts with the Deceased* (awarded a 2023 Scientific and Medical Network book prize). Project leader of an international research project on the Phenomenology and Impact of Spontaneous After-Death Communications. Founding and current member of the Board of Swiss IANDS (International Association for Near-Death Studies).

"One of the best lectures I've ever attended was given when I was a student nurse, over thirty years ago. The topic was *Sexually Transmitted Diseases*, and the lecturer was Dr Anona Blackwell, and it was delivered with such enthusiasm and passion that I was captivated throughout and to this day, still recall key information discussed. Now retired, consultant physician, medical educator and eminent researcher Dr Blackwell bravely comes out of the spiritual closet in her fascinating memoir *From Medic to Mystic* which depicts the span of her highly successful medical career. Amongst many accolades, Dr Blackwell has published many papers on her medical research in The Lancet, was a member of The Royal College of Physicians Integrated Health Committee and has met HRH King Charles.

In her book, Dr Blackwell unabashedly shares her very sacred and personal spiritual experiences. Very few others of her professional standing would have the courage to publicly admit to such experiences. It is Dr Blackwell's passion for promoting a more holistic side to medicine that is the motivation to share this with others. Dr Blackwell describes some early childhood experiences which were later superseded by her scientific medical training. When Dr Blackwell's spiritual path opened up during the latter stages of her career, she was on a quest to understand her experiences in more depth and in turn be of further benefit to her patients as she was able to apply this in appropriate ways to her clinical work as a consultant physician.

In the appendix, Dr Blackwell has included her essay on how she predicted medicine would look 100 years in the future. Not surprisingly, some of her predictions have come to fruition including the pandemic. This book gives hope for a more integrated and holistic approach for future medicine. Not only did Dr Blackwell make a valid contribution to healthcare during her career but continues to do so in her retirement with this book.

When I reflect on the book, I can't help but think how lucky patients were to be treated by such a kind-hearted and open-minded consultant and I imagine that many medical students and colleagues have been inspired and positively influenced by her to take this into future medical care. What a refreshing book to read, I thoroughly recommend it."

— PENNY SARTORI, PhD, Senior Lecturer in Adult Nursing,
Swansea University, author of *The Wisdom of Near-Death Experiences*

"Inspiring. Insightful. Delightful. *From Medic to Mystic* is a rare combination: clear stories of extraordinary personal psychic experience, the impersonal perspective of a highly trained medical professional, shared by someone who made me laugh out loud."

— JOSEPH SELBIE, author of *The Physics of Miraculous Healing*"

FROM MEDIC TO MYSTIC

The True Story of an
Academic Physician's Journey
Into the Paranormal

Anona Blackwell
BSc, AKC, FRCP

© Anona Blackwell 2025

All rights reserved. No part of this book may be reproduced by any mechanical, photographic, or electronic process, or in the form of a phonographic recording; nor may it be stored in a retrieval system, transmitted, or otherwise be copied for public or private use—other than for "fair use" as brief quotations embodied in articles and reviews—without prior written consent of the publisher.

Disclaimer

The statements made by the author and any recommendations of services in this book are not intended to diagnose, treat, cure or prevent any disease. The information provided and knowledge and experiences shared by the author are not intended to be a substitute for professional medical advice, diagnosis, or treatment.

ISBN 978-1-0685110-0-4

Edited by Sandra Sedgbeer
Cover and interior design by Damian Keenan
This book was typeset in Adobe Garamond Pro with Cochin and ITC Century Std Book Condensed used as a display typeface.

You can get in touch with the author of this book using the contact form on her website at www.drblackwell.co.uk

Published by
Archeus Books

Contents

Author's Note 9
Acknowledgements 11
Introduction 13

PART ONE:
TREADING THE ORTHODOX PATH

1. The Early Years 17
2. A Baptism of Bombs and Fire—My Time at St. Stephen's 30
3. From the Middlesex to St. Thomas' 42
4. Mount Pleasant & Singleton Hospitals, Swansea 53

PART TWO:
DOWN THE RABBIT HOLE

5. Into the Alternative 63
6. The Power of Prayer 74
7. Meeting the King 87

PART THREE:
FOLLOWING THE YELLOW BRICK ROAD

8. The Boy Who Walked Through the Wall
   and Other True Stories 95
9. Close Encounters of a Furred and Feathered Kind 107
10. Psychometry Part One 121
11. Psychometry Part Two 133

12. What I *Know* Vs. What I *Believe* About the Paranormal:
    PART ONE: What I *Know* is Real 151
13. What I *Know* Vs. What I *Believe* About the Paranormal:
    PART TWO: What I *Believe* But Do Not (as Yet)
    Know is True 165

PART FOUR:
THROUGH THE LOOKING GLASS

14. Global Chaos, the Paranormal, and the Concept of Wetiko 187
15. From The Lancet to the Light—Reflections on My Journey 201

EPILOGUE 213
APPENDIX I - Reflections on Medical Advances 2007-2107 215
APPENDIX II - HRT is for Women Who go Mad
    at the Menopause 225
APPENDIX III - Anam Cara 228

Recommended Reading 229
About the Author 238

Author's Note

To my best recollection, all events and personal stories in this book are factually correct. In many circumstances, I made contemporaneous notes of what happened and tried to describe the experiences chronologically, making the narrative easy to follow. Except where I have permission, minor changes have been made to some names and locations to protect the individual's identity.

Acknowledgements

My thanks to the following people who directly and indirectly helped incarnate this book:

Professor Jean Hanson, FRS, my late tutor in the Biophysics department at Kings College London, for having faith in my abilities from our first meeting, for acting as my academic mother, and for helping me obtain a place at medical school as a graduate entry student when such places were hard to find. I cried for three days when she died in 1973 because, without her, I doubt I would have had the courage to undertake a second degree. I hope we meet again.

My old school friend **Susan Heathcote**, for being the font of all knowledge of Abergavenny past and present, and who gives of her time to help with people's problems, from finding a reliable plumber to locating the obituary of one of our grammar school teachers whose death I had predicted almost 60 years ago.

Jane Hutchinson, an incredible medium and friend who graciously explained how mediumship works and for allowing me to chair her joyful Sunday spiritual meetings in Hereford.

Lynne McTaggart, whose book, *The Field* helped save my sanity when my scientific brain could not accept/process the paranormal events I was experiencing.

Sandie Sedgbeer, my editor, for supporting me during times of stress and grief and moulding me from an 80s Lancet-style academic author to a writer of a very different genre.

Professor Charles Tart, for kindly allowing me to re-publish his Western Creed.

My parents, for providing a safe though challenging childhood; my numerous **friends and colleagues** for their support and never doubting my sanity; and **my dogs**, for trying to teach me unconditional love and how to live in the moment—an ongoing project.

Finally, I extend my heartfelt gratitude to my **former patients**, from whom I learned so much—especially those who enrolled in my study on using metronidazole to treat anaerobic/bacterial vaginosis—and who gave freely of their time, never realising how many millions of lives they would help improve.

Introduction

On February 10th 2007, The Lancet asked its readers who work in health care to submit a fictional short story on "any aspect of medical science or health—past, present, or future"—for a competition. The successful essay would be published in its end-of-year special issue.

I decided to write a largely fictional piece set in the year 2107, imagining how medicine had developed over the previous century. I combined some of the more esoteric research, knowledge, and information I had been exploring—much of which I deemed unlikely to be familiar to my colleagues in the orthodox medical community—and allowed my imagination to trace things forward from there.

But I never submitted my entry.

Why?

As a respected academic doctor with the highest credentials and three Lancet-published papers, I was afraid my peers would consider me mad for having such fanciful, radical ideas.

Fast-forward sixteen years to early 2023. Having completely forgotten about the essay, I was astounded when I chanced upon it whilst clearing out some files and realized how prescient I had been. I had even predicted a global pandemic some twelve years before COVID-19 occurred! Since it epitomises how my life has been quite literally a dance between what the mystic and writer Carlos Castaneda called ordinary and non-ordinary reality, I have included it in Appendix I.

Although that essay was partly fiction, the main body of this book is autobiographical. It describes how, after experiencing many anomalous incidents, I spent years trying to make sense of them and morphed from being a scientifically trained Medic into a Mystic who cannot deny that there is so much more to us and to life than we currently understand.

The paranormal events you will read about in this book all occurred. There are many more that I don't have the space to share here. Instead, I will post them on my website and invite others to share their experiences.

We live in a time of exponential scientific advances in our understanding of human, animal, and even plant consciousness. Artificial Intelligence (AI) is also becoming part of our everyday lives, blurring the boundaries between what is real and what is virtual. As a result, we risk losing our connection with nature, Spirit, real people, and the essence of our humanity.

Over the years, many people, including several eminent professionals, have told me about their incredulous stories but feel they dare not publicly disclose them. I hope my decision to write about my excursions into non-ordinary reality will encourage others to reveal their paranormal experiences and not feel they may be considered crazy.

PART 1

TREADING THE ORTHODOX PATH

CHAPTER 1

The Early Years

I was 22 when I first became aware I had a clitoris. I was in a practical anatomy class at medical school, and I had just been asked to hack off the penis of a very well-endowed corpse. We had been divided into teams of six and allotted a body to work with. I was the only female in my group, and since none of the boys would do it, the gruesome task was left to me. After removing the organ an instructor showed me how to cut the penis lengthwise so that the second team allotted to that corpse could examine it and learn its anatomy. We were then transferred to a female corpse that was being dissected by an adjacent group. That's when I discovered the clitoris.

Having previously had no idea I had a clitoris, I raced home to get a mirror to see if I had some congenital abnormality. But no, there it was, sleeping silently where it always had been, unloved and untouched like an orchid hiding under a leaf in the Amazon rain forest. And thus, with just a few ultimately traumatic excursions into male territory, it was to remain.

Looking back on that episode of enlightenment, I think it's fair to say that I've always been somewhat... unconventional. Quirky and eccentric, and considered a nerd at school, it was clear from the outset that I was never going to be a conformist. I had too much curiosity, doggedness, and what the Native Americans call "the coyote trickster" sense of humour to quietly comply with the obligatory customs, rules, or styles of any cultural group or institution.

Maybe that's why I am one of the few Lancet-published scientist/physicians who has no reticence in confessing they've not only had psychic and paranormal experiences since childhood, but are just as happy to speak about their illuminating forays into complementary and alternative medicine, shamanic teachings, and energy medicine studies as they are about their accomplishments in genitourinary medicine, or the studies they undertook to earn the coveted BSc and FRCP postnominal qualifications.

But I digress. The stories I want to share with you will make much more sense if I begin at the beginning where it all started.

The magical journey that led me to international medical research fame, seeing the spirits of patients' late relatives and pets, diving down rabbit holes of studying consciousness, metaphysics, after-life communication, Ayurvedic medicine in India under the auspices of the former Prince's Foundation for Integrated Health, and ultimately meeting HRH Prince Charles in person (long before he was King) began in Abergavenny in 1949.

I was the younger daughter of Wyndham and Elsie Blackwell. Dad was a bus driver, and Mum a housewife/market gardener who later ran a fruit and vegetable stall in Abergavenny market. Our family home was just a ramshackle tin shack that had once been part of a temporary village set up in the early 1900s to house the men employed to build Grwyne Fawr Reservoir in nearby Forest Coalpit. Because the buildings were built of wood and corrugated iron it quickly became known as "Tin Town."

The inner walls of our tin shed were made of slatted wood, and with no insulation, the bungalow was very cold and damp. Icicles up to a foot long would form overnight inside bedroom windows and because we had no inside toilet, we had to keep a pot under the bed, so sometimes, even our urine froze. The coats on the bed and sacks on the floor provided little warmth, but we were content. We had a coal fire in the living room, and every Sunday we had a hot bath in a large tin tub, which Mum would drag inside to the small kitchen.

My sister and I would take turns having the first bath since my parents could only afford to heat one lot of water in the small galvanised electric boiler. There were no curtains in the kitchen, so Mum would use a dark green tablecloth to cover the window whilst we bathed. Life was not easy, and from infancy, I suffered recurrent ear infections, possibly made worse by my dear father's smoking. He used to blow hot smoke in my ears to ease the pain, an act of paternal love that nowadays would be considered abuse.

There was no internet back then, and we had no telephone or television. Since we lived a mile outside Abergavenny, we also had few friends with whom we could compare our lives. It was the best Mum and Dad could do. Our water supply came from a lake on an estate up the road, and in the spring, my sister and I were delighted when tiny tadpoles appeared in the *bosh** in our kitchen, whose tap was our only constant water supply. The council brought us drinking water in a horse-drawn tank pulled by a grey mare every few weeks. It was lovely seeing the horse, and Mum would give us a few carrots to feed it whilst the fresh water was unloaded into our galvanised tank. Likewise, we had no drainage other than a cesspit, which Dad would empty twice a year and spread the contents between rows of kale used to feed our cow. Nothing was ever wasted; scraps were given to our dog, grass clippings to the chickens, and our pig had what was left! Trips out would almost always be work-related. So in the early 1950s, when health and safety were not considered necessary, our relaxation

---

*   South Wales slang for a kitchen sink.

usually involved Dad, his beloved Fergie tractor and a wooden trailer he had constructed.

Sugar Loaf Mountain was just up the road from us, along the main A40, then up a lane to the top. Nowadays, there is a proper car park, but Dad would take us right up to the foot of the mountain where we would picnic next to a stream. We would make sandwiches with white bread and butter and bacon fried on a makeshift open fire beside the stream. I can still smell the burning heather Dad harvested to get the fire going. None of this would be legal nowadays, but the mountain was empty back then, apart from the birds and us. It was a paradise, although we did not know it.

After eating, Dad was always very strict about pouring lots of water on the fire, and we would all stare at the steaming ashes before work began. Mum and Dad would cut fern and load it onto the trailer for winter bedding for our cow, whilst my sister and I would collect sheep droppings for fertilising Dad's tomatoes. During September, our gran and grandad would join us on the Sugarloaf to pick wimberries for Mum's market stall. There would be no sheep dropping collection on those occasions, but we would gather as much fern as possible, given the number of people on the trailer.

Other memorable days out were when Dad harvested hay with his trusted Fergie and trailer. One year, the groundsman at Nevill Hall Hospital, just down the road from our home, asked Dad to clear away the hay he had cut. Built in the 1890s and used as a convalescent hospital in 1920, the hospital grounds were beautiful with large trees, lush rhododendron bushes, and a stream. My parents and grandad would load the hay whilst me and my sister would scamper off to look for watercress in the stream. The days were sunny, and the scents of the wildflowers and hay still linger as I recall the trip home on the top of the hay wagon along the Brecon Road. Massive horse chestnut trees lined the drive to the hospital and both sides of Brecon Road with the trees' branches meeting in the middle. We used to reach up and touch the leaves and duck when we passed a low-lying branch. Such days will never happen again, a prime example of the Welsh term *"hiraeth."**

The six-year age difference between my sister and me meant we had little in common. She was slim and artistic and into painting and playing the piano, whilst I was a plump tomboy, more interested in milking the cow or helping Dad grind the valves in our car. I was very close to the land, and as a five-year-old, I would spend hours just sitting alone by our beehives, quietly talking to the bees. I had a Spirit friend, a dark-haired little girl called Christina, whom I would play with and make my mum lay a place for at the table next to me. Mum thought it odd, not that I was constantly talking to Christina, but that I never asked for food to be put on her plate.

When I was eleven, Dad had a heart attack. A doctor had warned Mum that my father could drop dead at any minute. After that well-meaning curse from the white-coated "shaman," my mother was forever watching Dad for any signs of imminent death. She developed severe anxiety and depression, which lasted until Dad actually did drop dead in our field some fifteen years later.

One Sunday morning, whilst helping her prepare the food she said to me, "Go and see if your dad is alright." My father had spent a little too long in our outside toilet which was replete with the Daily Mirror torn into neat squares on a spike, and a candle and matches for nocturnal use. My mother was afraid that Dad was dead, and I was the go-between.

---

* *"Hiraeth"* is a Welsh word that has no direct English translation. It is an ephemeral, wistful yearning for past experiences and places.

"Pops, are you OK?" I whispered through the door.

"It's your mother worrying again. I am okay!" Dad replied crossly.

Dejected by my father's rebuke, I duly reported back to mum. A week later, the same thing happened, and fearful of another scolding, I stood at the wooden door of our outside (and indeed only) loo with its four-inch gap at the bottom for 1950s-style health and safety. But I could not see Dad's wellie boots moving.

"Dad ...?" I hesitantly enquired.

"What now?" He gruffly replied."

"Well ... I am peeling potatoes for Sunday dinner, and I just want to know if you are okay so we don't waste any potatoes." My father's annoyance turned into a fit of laughter and I skipped happily back to Mum with the good news. Thus began my lifelong retreat into comedy in the face of adversity.

Dad was a dowser and a self-taught electrician, mechanic, and mystic. Indeed, he was "some unsung, rustic polymath" if ever there was one. These facts may be relevant to what happened some months later when Pops had a second heart attack. As was the usual practice in those days, he was nursed in bed at home. One day, Mum and I noted that something strange was going on. Dad was not only cold and clammy to the touch, but he was also vibrating. In fact, his entire body was buzzing. We were completely mystified. There was no obvious explanation for this strange phenomenon.

"Well, I certainly don't vibrate when I join him under the eiderdown at night," Mum said.

"Then I think we should call his GP," I suggested. The call was duly made, the visit paid, but still no explanation was forthcoming. Days passed and dad continued to buzz. A second GP stopped by from the practice. But he didn't have a clue either. And so it continued until one day, Mum had a hair appointment. "Will you watch over your father?" she asked as she sailed out the door.

Intrigued by Dad's curious buzzing, I stood contemplating his juddering body when a bright idea suddenly popped into my head. *Perhaps all Dad needs is to be grounded!* I thought. Confident I could do that, I made a beeline for Dad's workshop. Rummaging around, I soon located a length of 13-amp electric cable, stripped the plastic off, and returned to my parent's bedroom, where I found Dad awake.

Ever the optimist, Dad good-naturedly agreed to let me wrap several feet of bare copper wire around his forehead and attach the other end to a metal spike. I thrust the spike into the garden outside his bedroom to earth him, and surprisingly, the buzzing ceased. Soon after, Mum arrived home. "Hello, what are you up to?" she enquired in a half-amused, half-quizzical tone that conveyed her befuddlement at how she and my father could have bred such an unusual child.

Whether it was the grounding that had helped Dad's recovery, I don't know, but curiously, some fifty some years later, grounding, also known as "earthing," is attracting considerable interest for its potential benefits in reducing inflammation, cardiovascular disease, muscle damage, chronic pain, and mood.

In fact, according to the late American Board-Certified Cardiologist Dr Stephen T. Sinatra, when done properly and safely, "grounding or earthing, may have profound effects on the autonomic nervous system (ANS), heart rate variability (HRV), and blood viscosity/zeta potential."*

Apparently earthing—the process of attuning to the earth's electrical potential—soaks up negatively charged electrons that neutralize free

---

* "How Earthing Benefits the Heart" by Stephen T. Sinatra, M.D., https://heartmdinstitute.com/alternative-medicine/grounding-healthy-heart/

radicals in our bodies and help stop cells from sticking together. Perhaps my father's red blood cells and platelets had clotted, blocking his arteries and causing inflammation which, in turn, had raised his free radicals, thereby encouraging more cells to stick together.

How a shy and isolated eleven-year-old could have intuited that grounding might benefit her father would have been as much a mystery to me back then as Dad's bizarre buzzing. But over time, I would learn that a precociously developed sixth sense wasn't the only gift in my metaphysical armoury.

Apart from his work on Red and White buses, Dad was also an excellent, albeit self-taught, electrician, who had wired all the houses my grandad had built in the 1930s. He also undertook contract potato planting with his Fergie tractor and potato planter.

In springtime, Mum and I would be bundled into the hopper of the planter and be driven to a farm at the foothills of the Sugarloaf to plant potatoes, popping a potato down the shoot every time the bell on the planter pinged. In retrospect, Dad was a shaman of sorts; he was an excellent dowser, could easily graft apples and pears, and was telepathic. As a young man, he would dowse around the houses that Grandad built in Cwmyoy to determine where to sink a well. He also had a telepathic link with me.

One day, when I was a medical student in the early 1970s, I noticed that a long-standing mole over my right scapula was bleeding. I had just completed a three-month stint attached to a firm where many patients had malignant melanomas, and, at first, I dismissed my fears, thinking I was overreacting because of all that I had seen. But my GP was very concerned and the mole was excised within a week at my local hospital. I hadn't told my family since there was little point worrying them until the histology report was available. The surgeon who saw me was a little annoyed that I had not been admitted for a general anaesthetic, and I sensed he felt it was a malignant lesion because he excised quite a large area of skin around the mole. Consequently, I was in a lot of pain that night. The following morning, I woke to find my landlord knocking on my door. Mum was on the phone. Dad had been awake all night with pain over his right scapula, and he knew it was my pain.

My main memories of my childhood are about working on the land, having recurrent ear and tonsil infections, being cold but well fed, and feeling very different from my peers. It was more than a feeling of being different because my fellow students actually lived in houses made with bricks. It was a feeling that I had almost nothing in common with them, as if I had come from a different planet and been abandoned here, giving me an inner sadness of the soul which has never left. This was highlighted when I was fifteen and the girls in my class were celebrating George Harrison's 21st birthday.

"Who is he?" I asked.

"The Beatles?!" They chorused, clearly bemused.

Years later, I was told by an old grammar schoolmate that I was regarded as a nerd, always to be found with my head in books rather than teenage magazines. I was extremely shy, and having had a stammer at infant school and not being able to read until I was eight years old, I had become a loner. I felt as if I saw the world through a different lens than my peers. It was no wonder I had only a few friends.

On Monday, February 20th, 1969, my first significant paranormal event occurred. I was a prefect and in charge of noting all the latecomers. The deputy headmaster and Latin teacher, Mr Harold Sharpe, worked with me whilst the rest of the school attended morning assembly. I was always keen to get to school but was very upset that morning and afraid to go. I told my mother that someone in school was going to die but I didn't know who it was. When I got to school, I told a few friends the same thing. But no one died. The following day, I was seized with the same extreme trepidation.

"Do you need to see a doctor?" Mum asked.

"No, he'll just think I'm crazy," I said miserably, trying to convince both Mum and myself that it must just be a severe case of unexplained anxiety.

Once again, no one died.

On the third day, I woke up feeling incredibly peaceful. "Mr Sharpe has died," I calmly announced to Mum.

"What?" Mum asked, intrigued but not quite believing it. Considering that we had no way of knowing if anyone had died, I couldn't really blame her. But then I went to school and heard the news that Mr Sharpe had died suddenly in his sleep.

Several months later, Mr Sharpe's wife who was one of my mother's customers, asked Mum if I would visit her house. She had heard about me predicting her husband's death and wanted to know if his Spirit was still in the house. A few days later, I was in her sitting room. "He's there," I said, pointing to a chair.

"I thought so," Mrs Sharpe calmly said. And that was it. No one said another word about that spooky experience.

There were no more predictions of death until many years later when I was working as a consultant in Swansea. But Mr Sharpe's predicted death was a milestone that foreshadowed the start of many paranormal events that followed over the years, whilst the death I was to foresee years later heralded a much more serious search into human consciousness.

Life continued to be hard. Six months before she was to go to Swansea University my sister left home to live with our grandmother, leaving me to take care of my depressed mother and poorly father.

Often in the summer, after school, I would be out on the land, weeding fodder beet or planting cauliflowers till it was dark. And since Mum had always maintained that education was the salvation of the working classes, I would stay up till 2:00 a.m. doing my homework.

Mum's philosophy was a maxim I was to take very seriously. I never went to parties since I felt no resonance with anything that wasn't work-related. Years later, Mum apologised for her oversight, saying she had taught me how to work but not how to play. Personally, I think it was just my nature.

One habit that may be of relevance to my burgeoning psychic abilities was that whenever I had a problem with homework, like Latin or Algebra, I would stand on my head with my feet pointing up my bedroom wall until the answer came to me. One day, Dad popped his head around the door and then quickly retreated when he saw me. "What on earth is she doing?" I heard him ask Mum.

"Oh, she's just doing her homework," Mum said.

Poor Dad, he must have thought I was quite odd, too. I didn't understand why I did it either. Until, almost sixty years later an idle Googling of the phrase "standing on your head and cognitive function" suggested I had been onto something.*

When I was eighteen, I moved to London to study biophysics at

---

* "Can Standing on Your Head Really Make You Think?" Daily Mail, October 21st, 2007.

Kings College, London. It was a modular system with various courses being taught at different campuses. My favourite subjects were those based in the biophysics department in Drury Lane, and my principal tutor/mentor was Professor Jean Hansen, FRS. I loved Jean and called her my academic mother until her untimely death three years after I qualified with an upper second honours degree. Jean saw in me something I never saw in myself and was instrumental in facilitating my life's path. She had arranged for me to undertake postgraduate study in America conducting research into a blinding disease called retinitis pigmentosa, but two dramatic things happened to nudge me on a different path.

The first started with severe chronic toothache and the surgical removal of a deeply impacted wisdom tooth. In lieu of a 21st birthday gift, my parents paid for me to have my wisdom tooth removed privately at St. Joseph's Hospital in Newport. Since this ensured I would sit my final exams pain-free, I gratefully agreed. When I woke up I was in great pain. The nurses were nuns and could not have been kinder. One of them gave me an injection of pethidine, which lifted my consciousness from intense torment to normality. I can remember thinking how good it must feel to ease someone's suffering, which made me wonder why I was doing academic research when I could help people more directly. I didn't know it then, but that planted a seed for what would come next.

Soon afterwards, I took a holiday job as a cleaner at Nevill Hall Hospital. One morning, I was polishing the floors outside a gynaecology outpatient clinic when I saw a young woman sitting in a chair, sobbing. When I asked if she needed anything, she blurted out that she had just learned that because of a pelvic infection, she would never have children. Feeling powerless to help because I was just a cleaner, I was comforting her as best I could when, suddenly, said seed began to germinate in my consciousness. Instead of going to America, I would ask Professor Hansen if she could support me in gaining admission to Westminster Medical School, where graduate entry students were accepted. And that is how, in the latter part of 1970, I became a medical student.

Little did I know that one day, I would not only publish a research paper in The Lancet on the prevention of pelvic infection—the very condition that had prompted my sudden decision to change course—but would also be invited by the Royal College of Obstetricians and Gynaecologists to participate in a closed workshop entitled "The Prevention of Pelvic Infection."

My parents had no money to support me and although I was able to get a grant, and somehow managed to survive on it, I seldom socialized at Medical School. I was determined to work hard. Five years later, in 1975, I gained my MBBS and started working at St. Stephen's Hospital in Fulham Road, West London.

CHAPTER 2

A Baptism of Bombs and Fire— My Time at St. Stephen's

In the first week of June, 1975, I arrived at the old St Stephen's Hospital in Fulham Road to begin my career as a doctor. Founded in 1878, the old part of St. Stephen's looked every inch a centenarian—tired, gaunt, and too worn down to repel the cockroaches that scuttled in the cupboards. The job was residential, and my room was located in a block just outside the main hospital. One dark, wet evening, as I ran from my ward to my room, I almost collided with a rain-sodden rat standing on its hind legs at the entrance, begging for sanctuary.

The walls of my room were so thin it was impossible not to hear everything that went on in the room next door. Richard, my neighbour, had the kind of good looks that ensured I would never forget his name, nor that he rarely spent a lonely night there. But since he is now a respected senior doctor, what happened in the room next to me at St. Stephen's shall remain there. Suffice to say, there were so many noisy nights when I would have to ring his room begging for peace that I'm sure I became his *coitus interruptus!*

My first working day at St. Stephen's began with a brief visit to the personnel department and a trip to the laundry room to collect a white coat. I stood patiently in line behind a fellow house surgeon on the same mission, excited to finally exchange my short, white student jacket for a proper full-length doctor's coat replete with my name on the collar.

"May I help you, doctor?" The laundry man deferentially asked my male colleague. All progressed well until it was my turn to proudly step forward. "Hello, luv. Domestic, is it?"

I felt like I had been outed as an imposter—as if he'd seen my fate had destiny not interceded. My mind instantly flew to an experience I'd had as a medical student on a teaching ward round. Most of my peers had come from private school backgrounds paid for by daddies who were themselves doctors. While making our ward rounds, the consultant noted that one of his patients had been born in Taormina and asked me where it was. I did not know and was mortified when he teasingly scoffed: "You don't know that after an expensive Roedean education?!"

When I had responded by announcing that I had attended a grammar school and that Dad was a disabled bus driver and Mum had a fruit and veg stall, the consultant looked shocked. I had morphed into my peer group but had curiously become an inverted snob; my pride at having overcome poverty to reach the same goal as my wealthier junior house doctors somehow made me feel strangely superior. With this in mind, I took a deep breath and responded to the laundry man in my poshest voice, albeit with a strong Welsh accent, "No. Actually, I am Mr MacFarlane's House surgeon."

"Oh, I am so sorry, doctor." The kindly laundry man said, clearly embarrassed. "How may I help?"

In those days, junior doctors had to complete six months of surgery and six months of general medicine before they were fully registered with the General Medical Council. Our working week at St. Stephen's was 120 hours of constant, on-your-feet-graft, often running long distances between the old and new wings, with overtime paid at 15 pence per hour after our 80-hours basic pay, which amounted to £2,859.00 per annum. And if we worked any less than 120 hours, my adored boss, Mr David

Aloysius MacFarlane, would question why we had taken time off! Over one Bank Holiday weekend, I clocked 56 hours non-stop during which there were five changes of nursing staff. It was dangerously mind- and body-crippling, and not all of us survived. At least one of my peers was forced to leave after developing severe colitis.

After one such marathon shift, I could barely stand. On returning to my room, I collapsed onto my bed, my body desperately yearning for rest. A few moments later, I saw my father enter the room. Then I heard the words, "Phone your mum!" He then disappeared into the wall. I was too exhausted to be curious about this apparent hallucination and just responded, "Dad, I am so tired, and Mum will be out in the field planting cabbages." Which she was indeed doing, as I discovered when the phone in my room rang just a few moments later. Wearily lifting the receiver, I heard a disembodied voice instructing me to Dial O for an outside call. We loved these calls since they usually signified that someone outside our hospital prison was contacting us. Only this time, the person reaching out to me was Robin, a friend of my Dad's. And he was calling to give me some news that was to change my entire life. My father had just died.

The sequence of events was revealed to me later. Mum, Dad, and Robin, a radiographer at our local hospital, had been busy planting cabbages when Mum decided it was time to make tea for everyone. She went indoors, put the kettle on, and let our German shepherd dog Lulu out. Lulu headed straight for the newly planted cabbages and immediately started running amuck. Dad turned, yelled at Mum, and then promptly dropped dead from a massive heart attack. Robin tried to revive him, but Dad was gone. His last duty on this side of the veil was to get his beloved wife some help. He found a way to contact me. Years before, Dad had made me promise to take care of Mum when he died. It was not a role I particularly relished as Mum was not the easiest of people to care for, but I considered it a sacred contract.

Dad's post-mortem visit was one of only two paranormal experiences I had whilst working at St. Stephen's. I suspect it was because the work was so gruelling that any ephemeral spiritual vibes got completely overwhelmed by the incessant noise of earth-based activity.

The second weird experience occurred just a few months later. Mum didn't cope well with Dad's death. She felt guilty that it was her fault for letting the dog out. The responsibility lay heavily on her, and she sank into such a deep depression, she was admitted to a psychiatric unit in Abergavenny where she had electroconvulsive therapy.

When Mum returned home several months later, she was pretty much penniless, Dad having loaned virtually all of his savings to someone who had not repaid him. Since I was not yet earning much, Mum had to work on her Abergavenny market stall to survive. It was gruelling work. Twice a week she had to get up at 6:00 a.m. and drive to Cardiff wholesale market to buy fruit and veg to supplement what she grew in our small market garden. Many times, she would cry in desperation. On one occasion, a few months after Dad had died, she phoned me at work, distraught because she had been crying so much she had crashed her car. I could not get compassionate leave and could only contact my aunt to help. I felt devastated but had to keep going, or my parents' sacrifices would have been in vain; I was not yet fully registered, and to drop out at that stage would have been a career-breaker. This event laid the scene for my second weird experience at St. Stephen's a few weeks later.

One of my colleagues was leaving and since it was my night off, I joined a doctors' mess party. At home we were teetotal, and whilst a medical student I was too poor to drink much. Indeed, the only time I had gone to the student's bar was on the day we received our results and the bar lady had initially refused to serve me because she didn't recognise me. I told her I had been there for five years. Because a close friend was leaving, I allowed myself to indulge in two large glasses of rather grim red wine. Next morning, nursing a bad hangover and feeling decidedly sick, I plodded listlessly behind my colleagues making the early ward rounds. I must have looked pretty rough because a friendly ward sister took pity on me and asked a senior house officer to prescribe something to ease my nausea.

An hour or so later, I was in the operating theatre waiting to assist my boss, Mr MacFarlane, with a fairly minor procedure, when I suddenly became unable to hold my head straight. I was having an adverse reaction to the medicine I had been given. Within seconds, I began to lose consciousness. Another junior doctor was hastily summoned to assist the boss as I was carried off to the post-op room. Suddenly, I was floating in another realm where everything seemed rather vague and cloudy. I could not see anyone, but I was aware of a divine, loving presence communicating with me. I don't recall any words being exchanged, but somehow, I knew that if I wanted to die now, I could. And if I decided to return, I would face a hard life. I had no idea where I was but I had no desire to leave this place. I felt so happy and comforted as if I was floating on warm, pink candy floss. Then I was "shown" the effect my death would have on my mother, and everything changed. I could not bear to hurt Mum when she had suffered so much after my dad's death so, reluctantly, I asked to be sent back and instantly, I was. The next thing I was aware of was the last drops of an intravenous dose of diazepam being slowly injected into a vein in my arm.

That was the nearest I have ever been to having a near-death experience (NDE). I didn't make very much of it at the time, though I did recall my father once telling me how he had almost drowned when he was a teenager and that his life had been played back to him when he was in another realm. Certainly, after my experience, I do not doubt that NDE's are real and give us a taste of the afterlife

Life as a junior doctor in the 1970s was very different from today. We worked outrageously long hours and were given much more direct responsibility for the forty ward patients under our care supervised by a registrar and a consultant. It was very scary, especially for the first few months when we transitioned from medical-student-book-heavy-learning to life-and-death-power over real suffering people. The analogy that occurs to me today is like playing a virtual war game and then suddenly finding yourself catapulted right into the front line of an actual conflict.

On one occasion, early in my first six months as a house surgeon, I saw a woman who'd been admitted as an emergency from Mr MacFarlane's morning outpatient clinic. She was in her late forties and had complained about rectal bleeding for over a year before her GP finally referred her to my boss. In those days, patients were admitted a few days before surgery to clear the bowel and do routine blood tests and a chest X-ray. I felt an instant connection with her; she was a mother archetype with which I resonated. And with Dad having recently passed, I was still finding it hard to control my emotions. My heart sank as I performed the rectal examination my boss had requested and felt a rock-hard mass which was now bleeding profusely on to my glove. I secretly shuddered; this lovely lady clearly had an advanced rectal tumour. My boss reiterated what a medical school professor had so often said: "If you don't put your finger in, you put your foot in." I was gutted.

The following day, I assisted my boss in the operating theatre as he conducted an exploratory laparotomy, which was our only means of making a firm diagnosis in those days. As Mr McFarlane opened up the patient's abdomen, we saw a mass of marble-sized yellow tumours all over the bowel and peritoneum. The liver was full of secondaries.

"There's nothing we can do," Mr McFarlane quietly stated, as he indicated he was going to start closing up the lady's abdomen. I wanted to argue with him, but there were hundreds of tumours, and I knew that only a miracle could save her.

The patient was still asleep on the ward when her mother and two twenty-something-year-old children arrived that evening to visit her. I had the responsibility of breaking the grim news. As I stood outside the small, womb-like room set aside for such a purpose, I felt extremely anxious, and my stomach was churning since I didn't know how to deliver such devastating news. What do you say? What words can possibly soften a prognosis that is going to ruin four people's lives? Finally, I couldn't leave it any longer and solemnly opened the door.

As I entered the room, the grandmother asked, "What did you find?" and I broke down into uncontrollable sobs. I didn't have to utter a single word; my tears told them everything they needed to know. We all sobbed for several minutes, hugging each other in our shared grief. Then my bleeper went off, and I had to hastily swallow my tears and rush off to another part of the hospital to see a lady suffering from a fit of hiccups.

As I choked out my goodbyes to the still-sobbing family, they begged me not to tell my patient what she had unless she specifically asked. A short while later, their loved one was transferred for terminal care, and I never saw her again. But still, the memory of that lovely lady lingers in my thoughts almost 50 years later. Even the newest recruit was thrown in the deep end in those days.

I had many traumatic experiences at St. Stephen's. One evening, I was part of the on-call surgical team when an eighteen-year-old Italian lad was brought to the Casualty department by ambulance. Handsome with a muscular body and beautiful black wavy hair, Antonio, who lived with his mum, had spent the evening out with friends and on his return had decided to have a bath before going to bed. But when he stood up to get out of the bath, he'd fainted and banged his head on the taps.

When I arrived at the Casualty department, I found Antonio lying on a trolley in a cubicle, separated from his mum by a curtain. His pupils were fixed and dilated and there were no heart sounds or pulse. I gently placed my hand on the site of the injury at the back of his head. His skull felt gritty, like broken egg shells, and when I pulled my hand away, a mixture of warm blood and brain tissue covered my fingers. When my registrar arrived to take over management of the young man's case, he ordered us to attempt to resuscitate the corpse, whispering that since the patient's mum was outside we must appear to have fought for the young man's life! It would give her some peace of mind. For fifteen minutes, we performed a simulated resuscitation. Eventually, my registrar left to break the tragic news to the young man's mother. Like the sensation of Antonio's broken skull, her wails will always be with me. No pain can be greater than that of a mother whose child has died, and in this instance, we admitted the poor bereft woman for the night so that sedation could at least buy her some time to process the true awfulness of what had happened. I still have haptic memory of that poor man's broken skull.

My job was what we called a one-in-two rota, meaning that we worked a nine-hour shift one day followed by a 33-hour shift the next. In addition, we had to cover other wards at night. Sometimes we could grab a few hours' sleep. But all too often we would be woken up to prescribe sleeping pills for an insomniac patient or attend to some other minor issue. However, we did have alternate weekends free and sometimes, when the sleep fairy had allowed us to rest, we even went out for a meal during the week.

One evening, on November 18th, 1975, after enjoying a rare night out with a non-medical friend, the phone in my room rang. Every off-duty doctor was immediately summoned to the Casualty department. It was the night of the Walton Street restaurant bombing, which killed two people and injured seventeen others. Rumour had it that one brave person had seen the sizzling bomb and had covered it with a soup tureen. All of us were nervous that more bombs might follow.

Casualty was frenetic with wailing patients, relatives, and distressed but amazingly focused staff. Even I, who would faint whilst taking a splinter from someone's finger, was able to cope with the blood and gore. One of my colleagues was inconsolable; a patient had just died in his arms from severe blood loss. I wondered if it was the person who had tried to cover the bomb. I counted myself fortunate that my late return meant that the most seriously injured patients had already been admitted and seen. Even so, I helped out in the operating theatres, all six of which ran through the night.

That was a grim night, lightened only in my memory by meeting a famous television comedian who was visiting one of the bomb victims. I say met, but in reality, he just smiled forlornly at me as we passed one another at the nurses' station; his on-screen bubbly personality muted by extreme distress. But that smile was enough to soothe my spirits and give me the strength to continue helping the injured. I thought of my granddad, who had fought and survived the carnage at Ypres in 1914, and wondered how he had coped.

Bombings were part of our normality. On October 23rd, 1975, I was off duty and lying up to my neck, relaxing in a large Victorian bath. The old part of St. Stephen's was blessed with these wonderful tubs, and it was one of the rare treats that made up for the long hours and daily coping with life and death situations.

A BAPTISM OF BOMBS AND FIRE—
MY TIME AT ST. STEPHEN'S

The warm water was a Welsh *cwtch*,* and I lay in it with a mud face mask newly plastered on my cheeks. Some ten minutes later, I heard a loud noise and wondered if it was a bomb. I could not run to Casualty since I would look like a victim with a muddy face and pink skin. Half an hour or so later, news trickled through that Professor Gordon Hamilton Fairley, a medical oncologist walking his dog outside his home in Kensington, had been killed when a car bomb intended for someone else exploded.

On another occasion, an IRA bomber blew himself up. His injuries were serious though not life-threatening. Few of us who had been there on the night of the Walton Street bombing wanted to treat him but we did as best we could, probably more than our best, because we were very aware of the need to observe our sacred contract as healers.

Years later, on March 30th, 1979, when I was working at St. Thomas' Hospital opposite the Houses of Parliament, I was with colleagues enjoying our mid-afternoon tea break when we heard a loud thud. "It's a bomb!" declared one of the doctors who was in the Royal Army Medical Corps. My mind immediately flew back to the night four years before when taking a bath at St. Stephen's; it was the same sickening sound. It was the bomb that killed Airey Neave, the shadow Secretary of State for Northern Ireland. Like most people, I felt outraged at the slaughter of the innocent. Some years later, when Mum and I visited Ireland and saw the prisons and places where the potato famine had unnecessarily caused widespread famine and death, I gained a greater understanding of the actions of its latter-day militants—though I could not approve of them.

Life at St. Stephen's was not all bombs and blood; it did have moments which, in retrospect, were darkly humorous. One day I was on a ward

---

* *Cwtch* is a Welsh word for cuddle or hug.

round with my fellow house officer—a registrar who I thought was very hot—and my avuncular consultant physician, Dr Philip Harvey. Together, the group was known as a firm, and our firm had just taken on a new patient who had been transferred from a surgical on-call firm. The patient was on my list, but I had not yet had time to see her. The ward round was in the new wing of St. Stephen's, which had a few single rooms and several four-bedders. Halfway through the ward round we were reviewing patients in a four-bedder and I was presenting a patient's details to the boss. Such times were sacrosanct and no one dare interrupt the consultant. Suddenly, a staff nurse scurried up to me and said she needed to give me an urgent message in private. The boss was not amused. I excused myself and took the agitated nurse aside. "What's up?" I asked, thinking it had to be something urgent to pull me away from my rounds with the consultant.

"That patient recently transferred has just set fire to three rooms, including the main patient's sitting room," she whispered. "I thought I'd better tell you rather than call the fire brigade, as she's your patient."

"FIRE!" I yelled as I rushed off, hot on the heels of the nurse, who by now was attacking the fire alarm with her soft ward shoe. Grabbing a fire extinguisher, I slammed it against the glass cover of the alarm just as several of my colleagues came pouring into the room, along with my hot registrar, who, without stopping to think, immediately aimed a water-based extinguisher at the television. Screaming at him, I shoved a carbon dioxide extinguisher at him whilst simultaneously grabbing my boss's arm to prevent him from switching the light on and possibly cooking my registrar before my secret, passionate plans had a chance to come to fruition. (They never really did. Well, not enough to make a story worth telling.) It was all over very quickly once the hot registrar aimed the water-based extinguisher at the burning curtains, while the rest of my colleagues were putting out the small fires my pyromaniacal patient had not so thoughtfully lit in the two other rooms. Next up, a pack of burly firefighters arrived and the arsonist was taken to a secure unit.

In 1976, as my year of long hours and extreme stress at St. Stephen's was drawing to a close, my bereaved mother started pressuring me to move back home to Abergavenny to train as a general practitioner. But I was not keen to leave London yet. Fortunately, fate stepped in one day when a solicitor friend, Kirran, called to say she had met an arrogant and self-opinionated public school-educated barrister named Alistair, whom she was convinced I would adore.

And here's where I get to confess that whilst I am very good at some things—making excellent mint sauce and fabulous marmalade, and even welding metal gates—when it comes to choosing the men in my life, I am shamefully ill-equipped. No, let's tell the truth; I am worse than hopeless. For some reason, I have always been attracted to those who ought to come with the warning "Danger! WMD" (Weapons of Mass Destruction to my emotions) stamped across their foreheads. As you've probably guessed, Kirran was right. Alistair was not just one of those WMDs; he was a purebred, veritable king among WMDs. And I was soon besotted.

Instead of joining my mother back in Abergavenny, I completed my year at St. Stephen's, moved into Alistair's house in South London, and obtained a senior house officer post in Genito-urinary medicine at the Middlesex Hospital. And in the few hours I wasn't practising medicine, I diligently focused on my other job as a Stepford-wife-in-training to Alistair. Thus, I moved on to the next chapter of my journey to spiritual awareness.

CHAPTER 3

From the Middlesex to St. Thomas'

In 1976, I moved to the Middlesex Hospital as a Senior House Officer (SHO) in the genitourinary medicine (GUM) department at James Pringle House. The brainchild of the father of UK genitourinary medicine, Dr Duncan Catterall, our department was the first GUM unit in the UK. A war hero, Duncan was an ideal teacher for junior staff learning the ropes. An old-style doctor who always insisted that we adhere closely to his departmental treatment protocols, he had a charming manner and was always immaculately dressed.

I had initially applied for the post because it was an easy option with no on-call or weekend work, which allowed me time to take care of the domestic duties that came with living with a man in those unenlightened times when everything in the home was largely considered a woman's purview. Curiously, Alistair was enlightened in that regard. But I was not, and had a fixed idea of female domestic duties. When my services were not required, I could visit my mother, who was still recovering from electroconvulsive therapy.

Whilst my time at the Middlesex was unremarkable in spiritual terms, I soon realised that the speciality fitted my academic background and idiosyncratic sense of humour like a glove. It was the pre-AIDS era when even hepatitis B was still known as Dane particle syndrome. Most conditions we saw, except for hepatitis and Herpes simplex infection, were treatable, and it was a rewarding speciality to work in. I was, however, a little bored. My undergraduate degree in cell biology/biophysics was as much about gaining knowledge as performing laboratory experiments, problem-solving, and creating hypotheses whilst my medical training was more about rote learning, making diagnoses, and following management protocols. The two mindsets were not always at ease with each other and, like a carpenter stranded on a desert island looking for bits of wood that he could carve into something of use, my inner academic was always looking for puzzles to solve. I did not have to wait long to find my own piece of wood.

When women came to a GUM unit for a check-up in the mid-1970s, they were tested for syphilis, gonorrhoea, trichomonas and candida infections as routine. We knew very little about chlamydia then, and routine laboratory tests for it did not exist. Another widespread infection was anaerobic/bacterial vaginosis (BV), which caused a fishy-smelling vaginal discharge. BV was not even recognised as a clinical entity, so it also went untreated. This was all to change when a chance comment eventually led me into over 25 years of research, which started at St. Thomas' Hospital and resulted in two Lancet papers. One of these papers established the specific abnormal bacterial vaginal flora associated with BV. The second confirmed that metronidazole was an effective treatment, allowing the drug to be awarded a UK product license for this condition. What was the chance comment?

One afternoon, I saw a young woman at the Middlesex who had been seen several times previously. She complained bitterly that her partner said she smelled like an old tin of anchovies. Yet all our tests, especially those for *Trichomonas vaginalis* (TV), which can also cause a smelly discharge, were negative. We used to look for TV on what we called a wet mount preparation which comprises one drop of vaginal secretion mixed with one drop of saline on a glass slide topped with a cover slip. TV looks like an amoeba with a tail and is very distinctive. I noted masses of motile bacteria were also present in most TV cases, but these were not considered significant. Indeed, many had not been categorised or even named at the time. I did not know what to do for this poor lady since her secretions were indeed very unpleasant, but the routine tests were normal. I asked the senior registrar for advice. He came to see the patient with me and advised that nothing was abnormal, adding that it was okay for women to smell fishy! I could not wait to get home and sniff my knickers which, as I suspected, were more or less odour-free. After a few moments of cognitive dissonance, I decided either my senior registrar's wife had a problem, or I did. Or the accepted definition of normal vaginal secretions was wrong. It was a defining moment in my life.

In 1977, after 18 months as Senior House Officer at the Middlesex, where I had gained a diploma in GUM, I was head-hunted for a GUM registrar post at St. Thomas' Hospital in London. I remained there until 1985, rising through the medical ranks from junior registrar to senior registrar, and finally to lecturer in a new academic unit.

My years at St. Thomas' were busy ones. I enjoyed my work and felt I was progressing well in my career. Alistair and I had settled down into a comfortable routine and enjoyed living together. Or so I thought... until April 1979, when I woke up one morning to the devastating news that Alistair wanted me to move out. He had been having an affair with a woman he had met at the Victorian Society and I was now surplus to requirements. I was heartbroken. We had been together for three years, and I had naively thought we had a good relationship. It took me a long while to get over the shock of Alistair's betrayal and the way he had abruptly dumped me.

Of course, if Alistair had married me, I would never have pursued the academic life, and millions of women who later benefitted from the refocusing of my sexual/nesting energy into my research work would not have been helped. I also suspect that my earlier bond with Spirit and my psychic abilities might not have flourished as well as they did once freed from the distractions of a live-in relationship. As it was, it didn't take long before I could once again combine orthodox practise with the sixth sense I had been born with.

The memory of my encounter with the woman at The Middlesex Hospital, whose malodorous problem was deemed normal, had stayed with me. I'd also become increasingly aware that, though common, these symptoms were not recognised as a clinical entity, and I became obsessed with the microbial flora of the vagina.

In 1978, I read a paper in the New England Journal of Medicine by Pheifer and colleagues describing an organism then called *Haemophilus vaginalis*, which, with anaerobic bacteria, seemed to be associated with vaginitis. The authors had also noted that an antibiotic, metronidazole, commonly used to treat *Trichomonas* infection, seemed to cure the condition. After reading this, I approached my GUM boss, Dr David Barlow and the head of the microbiology department, Professor Ian Phillips, to see if we could repeat the work of Pheifer's group. I wanted to define more precisely the anaerobic flora present in the vaginal secretions of affected women. Professor Phillips asked one of his colleagues, a senior laboratory technician named Elizabeth Taylor, to lead the investigation of the microbial flora whilst I provided the clinical samples.

In 1982, our paper was published in The Lancet. It confirmed that women with non-specific vaginitis (as it was then known) did indeed have an abnormal vaginal flora in which the usual *lactobacillus flora* was replaced by one of mixed anaerobic bacteria and a facultative anaerobe called *Haemophilus vaginalis*, which was later renamed *Gardnerella vaginalis*. We then secured funding from a drug company to carry out a formal double-blind, placebo-controlled study of the use of metronidazole to treat the condition. Ethical committee approval was also forthcoming since having become a well-established safe drug to treat *Trichomonas*, our study would just extend the indications for its use.

I designed the protocol for the study, which included a list of inclusion and exclusion criteria. It was very time-consuming and involved a lot of work. Patients were recruited from infected women who attended my busy routine clinics. When a suitable patient gave written consent to entering the study, she was asked to reattend when my laboratory co-worker would prepare and bring all the necessary culture plates to assess a plethora of bacteria. Follow-up appointments were arranged around patients' menstrual cycles and many other factors, so the timing was crucial. Compliance was essential as funding for the laboratory technician was time-limited. With mobile phones still very much in the future and many patients reluctant to divulge their contact details, we were constantly on tenterhooks; if even one patient failed to reattend for an appointment, hours of work would be wasted, whilst too many non-attenders would result in our study losing its statistical significance.

With so much at stake, I was driven to pull out every tool in my armoury—including my belief in the power of prayer. So it was that the day before each patient's appointment, I would hold their notes in my hands and say a prayer over them, visualising their presence in my clinic the following day. The treatment worked so well that we stopped the study after 40 patients since every woman, bar one, who received treatment was cured, whilst there wasn't a single cure among those in the placebo arm.

The Lancet is a prestigious journal and a game-maker for change in clinical practice. After our paper was published, I became a recognized international expert on this condition. When I subsequently lectured overseas, I was often treated like a rock star, with professors asking me to sign copies of my article and be photographed with them. Since some studies lose statistical significance if there are too many non-attenders, one professor was eager to know how I achieved such good patient compliance. It was a surprise even to me. But since I couldn't tell the professor about my praying, I put it down to our good fortune in having a reliable patient group.

As for the lone woman who failed to reattend, I wasn't surprised; my intuition had already flagged her as the most likely patient to let us down. In fact, because of that, I had tried desperately to find a reason to exclude her, but my clinical and scientific training wouldn't allow that.

During the study, my prayers were seriously tested when, on one occasion, our technician said he could not make an agreed appointment. Upset because we did not have the patient's contact details, I took her notes into my office, and prayed for her to phone me so I could rearrange her appointment. It worked, and soon afterwards, I received a phone call.

"You have been trying to contact me," the lady stated, matter of factly. Apparently, we both regarded telepathy as normal. When she attended her appointment, I asked her to speak to my boss, the late Dr Nicol Thin and tell him what had happened. Whilst I knew I was regarded as a conscientious worker, I was concerned that my colleagues might see me as an eccentric. Since this patient was both delightful and very articulate, I felt her speaking to Nicol would help him understand that I wasn't so unusual after all. Nicol was an ex-army, no-nonsense sort of guy, but he was also very supportive throughout my career.

Another weird thing happened during my time at St. Thomas' when I was admitted to the hospital with a crippling attack of sciatica for which I was given epidural morphine. One day while my mother was working on her market stall in Abergavenny, she got into conversation with a complete stranger who told her that she could "see that her daughter was in hospital with severe pain in her left buttock."

"I'll pray for her," the stranger had promised.

A few days later, I awoke one morning to the sight and sounds of three large ravens fluttering near the ceiling above me. A few seconds later, they flew away through the window … which was completely closed. Almost instantly, my back pain started to ease and I could walk again, although it took another three months, and several acupuncture sessions before I could return to work. At the time, I put the hallucination down to the painkillers. But as life took me further into realms of the paranormal, I began to think otherwise. Years afterwards, I was to have an even more remarkable encounter with birds. But we will get to that a little later.

I had many telepathic experiences whilst I was a consultant in Swansea, some of which are described in Part Two. But here are a few incidents that support my belief that we have access to far greater powers and abilities than we imagine.

Whilst I was still a medical student, I was invited to attend a dinner party one evening with a bright American friend, named Tobias, who came from a well-respected military family and was doing a PhD in War Studies. The dinner party was hosted at a rather posh London flat belonging to friends of Tobias's father. I was awed by the old-world ambience of the flat, which looked like something straight out of an Agatha Christie novel with its abundance of cut glass and mahogany. I felt like Alice in Wonderland; it was so different from the tin shack I had grown up in.

Looking back on it now, the entire evening felt as though it was taking place in another dimension. The host and hostess were very kind and welcoming, even though I was certain I must have appeared to them like a child on its first visit to the seaside. Especially when the starter—an avocado—was placed in front of me and I asked what it was. I had never seen an avocado before.

Toby was seated opposite me, and another young man who I had never met before, was placed on my right. I couldn't help noticing that this young man seemed rather anxious. Throughout the meal, he kept mumbling about his treatment for nonspecific urethritis (NSU). He was afraid the tablets he was taking would not work and that his girlfriend might leave him. The intensity of his angst affected me so much that I couldn't stop myself from trying to put his mind at rest. So when we left the dining room for coffee, I whispered to him, "Don't worry about your NSU, just complete the antibiotics, you will be fine, and your girlfriend will forgive you. Say you were drunk!"

The young man's face was a picture of abject horror. "How do you know I have NSU?" he demanded. "I haven't said a word to you about it." I then realised that being placed so closely within his energy field, I must have unconsciously telepathically tuned into his thoughts, which I'd mistakenly interpreted as speech. I fear my dining companion may have spent the rest of his life afraid that all women could read men's minds.

Several other spiritual events of note occurred during my nine years at St. Thomas'. But first, let me set the scene so you can understand what happened in context.

By the early 80s, I was beginning to get an international reputation for my academic work but was still a junior doctor at a prestigious London teaching hospital. We wore white coats, carried stethoscopes, and consultants formally supervised our units. There were three shifts of open-access male and female clinics each day. One day, I had just arrived for my afternoon female clinic when a male colleague who was leaving for his lunch break asked me to prescribe treatment for a lady he had just diagnosed as having a yeast infection. The patient was a well-dressed woman about ten years my senior. I explained the diagnosis and gave her some pessaries. She was just about to leave when, suddenly, the room was suffused with a golden light. To my right, I could see an egg-shaped energy field surrounding what I can only describe as a lady radiating intense love. The feeling of love and grace was so palpable that it's been impossible to forget. As the patient reached the door, the light began to diminish, and I felt an overwhelming urge to ask her to sit back down and tell her what I had seen. When I did, she immediately broke down in sobs, saying she was head of English at a private school and after her mother had died a few months earlier she too had seen what I had witnessed. But she was afraid to tell her GP for fear she would be deemed insane and lose her job.

I gently explained how loved ones never die, that her mother was always near her, and had appeared to me so I could comfort her daughter. I gave her the address of the Spiritualist Association of Great Britain so she could talk to someone there and perhaps book a session with one of their trained mediums. Before she left, she hugged me and said I had saved her sanity. I never saw her again, but I felt very privileged. This woman had come to the clinic seeking treatment for a physical condition, and I'd been able to offer her emotional solace as well.

On a more humorous note, some spiritual experiences can be quite funny. One such example happened during a female clinic in the early 80s. My patient, who was in her late 40s, complained of a severe vulval itch. She was an archetypal, salt-of-the-earth, working-class cockney with an accent like a female version of Michael Caine. I introduced myself and began to interview her. I started by checking I had the correct case notes by asking her full name, etc. Then, all of a sudden, I became aware of a strong male presence in the room. In ordinary reality, the room was empty apart from a desk, two chairs, an X-ray monitor and us. But in my reality, a rather disgruntled man was also present. Feeling somewhat intimidated by his presence, I turned to my patient, and without stopping to think whether she might be alarmed, calmly told her that I couldn't ask her any more intimate questions as there was a man in the room with us.

"Oh, don't worry, Doc," the lady said in her lovely cockney accent. "It's only Arthur, my late husband. He's a bloody nuisance, he follows me everywhere. Just tell him to bugger off and carry on." So, I did. And no doubt realising that he'd been rumbled, Arthur duly buggered off when I started asking questions about his wife's symptoms and sex life.

Minor psychic experiences whilst at St. Thomas' seemed to increase as I spent more time on my own. On one occasion, a beautiful young woman came to see me. Louise was a musician and I could sense many spirits around her. When I related what I had seen, she told me she was an up-market medium, and her fee was £80 an hour, which was a massive amount in those days.

St. Thomas' teaching hospital was then, as now, a centre of excellence in orthodox medicine and I thrived in this academic environment. As an internationally acknowledged expert in my field, my colleagues, some of whom were aware of my intuitive abilities, apparently accepted my eccentricities and open-minded beliefs.

Anomalous phenomena have baffled us since time began. While science still has not identified how they work, several rigorous studies have provided sufficient evidence that phenomena such as extrasensory perception (ESP) and telepathy are real. Indeed, one story that used to surprise my students reveals the role that telepathy played in the invention of electroencephalograms (EEGs).

In 1892, a nineteen-year-old German cavalryman named Hans Berger narrowly escaped death after falling off his horse in the path of a moving gun carriage. Miraculously, the heavy gun carriage was stopped in time, leaving Hans shaken but alive. Berger's family lived many kilometres away, and he could not let them know of his accident. So you can imagine his shock when a telegram arrived from his sister inquiring about his well-being. Stunned by how his sister, with whom he had a close relationship, could have known his life had been in peril, Hans Berger could not get the incident out of his mind. After military service, he studied medicine and later trained as a psychiatrist. He then went on to research the electrical activity of the brain. In 1924, Hans Berger recorded the first electroencephalogram (EEG). EEGs remain one of our primary medical diagnostic tools today.

By 1985, my research at St. Thomas' was over. My nine years there had been a marathon of long hours and hard work balanced by the camaraderie and support of a wonderful team of colleagues. I was invited to apply for a consultant post but I needed to move on. It had been six years since Alistair had left me, and I still longed for him to return my love. But he never did. I had waited long enough. Another love interest was calling me—my mother's Jack Russell puppy, Towser. Towser loved my mum but he worshipped me and I could not bear to be away from the canine love of my life. The time had come to move back to Wales where I would be nearer to Towser. So I applied for and obtained a consultant post in Swansea.

CHAPTER 4

Mount Pleasant & Singleton Hospitals, Swansea

The interview for my consultant post in Swansea occurred on a beautiful summer day in 1985. As Mum drove me to Singleton Hospital overlooking the sea, I was delighted at the sight of seagulls swooping over our heads.

As I entered the administration department's boardroom, I saw a single chair placed in the centre of a semi-circle of middle-aged men in suits. I was wearing a neat black dress with a jaunty bow tie at the neck.

"I hope you're not intimidated by being the only woman in a group of men," the chairman greeted me in a soft Welsh accent.

"It's seeing you all fully clothed that scares me," I nervously responded before hastily adding, "Well, in London, I see at least sixty half-naked men every day." I meant it as a joke, but I could see some men crossing their legs in fear. It was not the best start.

After reviewing and questioning me about my CV at length, they then asked if I could talk about something other than medicine for fifteen minutes. Since I had spent several years attending evening car maintenance classes, I opted to give them a description of how to carry out a routine car service. Around ten minutes in, just as I had got to explaining how to use feeler blades to set the gap on spark plugs, I noticed that the Chairman was looking a little bored. "Why are you giving up a top London job to move to Wales?" he interrupted.

"I have family commitments in Abergavenny," I replied, unwilling to say that, in truth, it was mainly motivated by my love for my mother's dog Towser, who had stolen my heart more than any man ever could.

I got the job, and in October 1985, I started my genito-urinary medicine consultant post in an old Victorian workhouse called Mount Pleasant Hospital in Swansea. The department was dark, the roof leaked when it rained, and some windows still had iron bars. It was a far cry from the modern unit I had worked at in London. But I never regretted moving home since the pain of not being near Towser was unbearable—second only to when he collapsed and died in my arms in 1999 at the age of 16.

My first clinic was a busy male session, and I felt thrown into the deep end when my senior colleague Dr Cobbold, left me to it. It was like trying to cook a five-course meal in someone else's kitchen. But all went well ... until a young man with urethritis was ushered into my office.

Having only been seen by my male predecessor, the patient was surprised to be greeted by a female doctor. When I asked him what was wrong, he said he had a discharge from his eye. I leaned forward to take a closer look at his eyes. "They look fine to me," I said after examining both eyes.

"Not that eye. This eye," he said, pointing to his crotch.

I was baffled... until one of my Welsh-speaking nurses explained that the Welsh word for eye, *"llygad,"* was also used to describe the urethral opening. That was the first of many lessons I received in Wenglish, or Welsh English.

It took me a few months to settle in and get used to being a consultant. As a junior doctor, there is always someone above you to ask, but when you become a consultant, you quickly realise that the buck stops with you. But I soon found local work colleagues who were eager to help. The head of the microbiology department, Dr David Joynson, was to become a long-term, supportive colleague and friend, especially when I wanted to carry out joint research projects. His colleague Dr Philip Thomas, the local chlamydia expert subsequently became a co-author in another game-changing Lancet paper published in 1993.

Overall, the routine work was relatively straightforward, and it wasn't long before I found myself looking for another challenge. My mother used to say I behaved like a caged lion when deprived of an intellectual outlet. She was right; I missed teaching, which had been an integral part of my work as a lecturer at St. Thomas'. I was thrilled when I was invited to lecture in Europe and offered two teaching trips to America. One was in Wisconsin, where I took part in making a teaching video with Professors David Eschenbach and Sharon Hillier, who were giants in their respective fields of gynaecology and microbiology. Back home, I also organized mini-conferences for local general practitioners and generally raised the profile of the Venereal Disease clinic from a backwater department in an old workhouse to first a centre for teaching and, later, for research of international repute. It would have been impossible without the help of the microbiology and gynaecology consultants and an incredible lady called Kathie Wareham, the director of the local clinical research unit.

My main problem was finding a clinical condition that ignited the same fire in my belly as when hearing that it was normal for women to smell fishy. Then, one morning, I saw a woman who'd had an abortion years before, which had been followed by severe pelvic infection and persistent lower abdominal pain. On performing a routine vaginal/pelvic examination, I felt a semi-fixed uterus that seemed stiff and lifeless. I felt compassion for my patient, who, in my opinion, had suffered so long from a disease that may have been preventable. The following day I spoke to a newly appointed consultant gynaecologist, Mr Simon Emery. I asked him if his speciality had specific guidelines for pre-surgical abortion infection screening/treatment. He said that none existed, and we discussed the possibility of a research project to see if pre-operative infection screening and therapy would reduce the rate of subsequent pelvic infection. The next step was to speak to Dr Philip Thomas regarding chlamydia detection. Philip, too, was keen to look into the problem. But I still needed someone to help get such a significant project up and running.

The dream of undertaking the study stayed with me. As I saw more patients with post-abortion infections, my concerns for future patients increased. Then, while attending one of the weekly grand rounds at Singleton Hospital, I had a chat with Kathie Wareham, who proved to be a major catalyst—and an eventual co-author—of a study that was eventually published in the Lancet in 1993.

I immersed myself in the microbiology of pelvic infection. Given my heavy clinical workload, it took several years to design the study, get ethical committee approval, conduct, and collect and collate the data. Finally, I booked three weeks of annual leave to write the paper. My co-authors helped with minor changes before we submitted it to the British Medical Journal (BMJ). To our disappointment, it was rejected. However, the reviewer suggested that it was "more Lancet material." My disappointment turned to joy when I received a letter from the Lancet agreeing to publish the work almost unaltered. My training in medical writing from Professor Ian Phillips at St. Thomas' had paid off. The Lancet has the highest impact factor in medicine, so I had good reason to be happy, and I hurried to give Simon the good news.

Soon afterwards, in 1993, my department was relocated to a new clinic based at Singleton Hospital.

Singleton Hospital 1993 to 2001

From 1993 to 2001, I was in a spiritual desert, devoid of any paranormal experiences and firmly locked in material reality. The move to new premises in Singleton gave me instant access to the library and its extremely helpful staff, laboratories, seminar rooms and, most importantly, my consultant and managerial colleagues. I carried out a few more treatment studies for anaerobic/bacterial vaginosis but, by then, I was best known for my work involving the prevention of pelvic infection.

I was asked to lecture at many venues within the UK, Europe, and the USA, and even took part in a BBC2 documentary about Chlamydia. But I missed the magic of my metaphysical experiences at St. Thomas'. I suspect my preoccupation with earth-bound matters had been so intense that the soft voice of Spirit went unheard.

In 1996, the Royal College of Gynaecologists (RCOG) invited me to participate in a closed workshop on "The Prevention of Pelvic Infection." The study group comprised twenty internationally acclaimed academics, mainly professors from the UK, Europe, and America. I was humbled to be included, but such is the prestige that accompanies publication in The Lancet that similar invites had become fairly common. Within the group, I was the only clinician working out in the sticks with a heavy clinical workload and no academic unit to support me. Participants were required to research a relevant topic to present at the meeting and then write it up as a chapter for the book that was to be published. As an added accolade, I was the only participant to be asked to present two different aspects of the pathogenesis of pelvic infection, so was doubly stressed.

In the eighteen months leading up to the workshop, I spent all my holidays and weekends conducting literature searches and writing my presentations. They had to be state-of-the-art because my peers were the best in their fields. I learned a lot about how stress affects the body during that period when I spontaneously started getting recurrent skin rashes, *urticarial vasculitis*, which would present as a feeling of intense localised heat. My body was dotted with painful lesions the size of my hand that stood about 3mm high and which gradually turned purple before disappearing, only to recur elsewhere on my trunk a few weeks later. I saw a dermatologist, but there was no specific treatment. Eventually, I discovered through experimentation that applying topical ibuprofen to one-half of the lesions resulted in more rapid resolution of the treated half. I never wrote it up, but this observation may plant a seed in the mind of a budding dermatologist.

At the same time, I also developed palpitations that occasionally made me feel as if I was dying. A 24-hour ECG revealed ectopic heartbeats, which remained abnormal right up until the day after my presentations when I miraculously woke up feeling well. My pulse was regular, my vasculitis had disappeared, and I had learned just how powerful our thoughts can be in causing illness.

I was delighted when my review of pre-abortion antimicrobial prophylaxis helped the group change the RCOG national guidelines. When they were later published in the RCOG's book "The Prevention of Pelvic Infection," I was pleased that the anger and sadness I'd felt on examining the patient with a "dead pelvis" so many years before had, with support from colleagues, been transmuted into action which helped permanently change the fate of thousands of women who subsequently underwent surgical abortions.

As my teaching and clinical commitments increased, my research work diminished. I was appointed vice chairman of Singleton Hospital's consultants' Committee in 1998 and was automatically made chairman in 2000. This role was time-consuming since membership in several other administrative committees came with it. I also got to meet the Minister of Health for Wales, and most of the senior consultants and managers, so my earthly street credibility was fully grounded and recognised by the powers that be. This stood me in good stead for the weird experiences which were to come when, on September 6th, 2001, I suddenly toppled completely down the rabbit hole and rediscovered a whole new alternative reality.

PART 2

DOWN THE RABBIT HOLE

CHAPTER 5

Into the Alternative

Ever since the unexpected (but fruitless) discovery of my clitoris, I had drifted mindlessly into a childless "motherhood" where long hours of studying, tending to patients, teaching students, caring for elderly relatives, and writing research papers filled the hole left by my hapless mother archetype. Year after year, my periods came and went at precisely 27-day intervals, largely uninterrupted by marauding spermatozoa. Each month brought a week or so of premenstrual angst, sometimes paralysing pain and bloody groundhog days.

Then, shortly after the millennium, I started to feel uncharacteristically tired and became plagued by insomnia. I was at the height of my professional career; I was chairman of my hospital's consultant committee and an active member of several other committees linked to the post. I was also a member of our clinical research group and had heavy clinical and teaching duties. Holidays were often spent lecturing or writing papers, caring for my 80-year-old mother, and maintaining our Abergavenny home. So, I put my fatigue down to my very unbalanced life.

My fatigue worsened, and I found myself in bed at seven-thirty every night for two years, yet I still could not sleep. My female patients empathised as hot flushes sent my face bright red and beads of sweat dripped from my fingertips. Luckily, we had a shower in my department, so whenever possible, I would take a shower instead of a lunch break so that I could at least change my underwear. A brain fog ensued, and I could only write half a page of notes before my arm gave way with muscle fatigue. I had to hold onto a chair or lectern when giving one of my two-hour teaching sessions to medical students and felt very depressed. I was in top form a year previously, giving a guest lecture to almost 2,000 delegates at an international infectious disease conference in Sicily. Now, I wanted to hide under my desk when even a single student sat in for tuition. It was the perimenopause from hell.

Then a few months before my 50th birthday, my ovarian biological clock abruptly ceased to tick. No more periods, not even a farewell sludge. Oestrogen receptors in my brain, muscles, eyes, skin, and everywhere else went cold turkey, and I felt very grim. I took solace in writing a short and amusing missive about my menopause, which The Lancet published in May 2001. (Since it summed up my menopause in a few paragraphs, I have included it in Appendix II.) Given the number of letters I received from doctors who had suffered similar problems and recent increased awareness of how bad the menopause can be, I know it is still relevant and, indeed, is still quoted.

This sudden proof that I was now officially post-menopausal also heralded my moving into my crone-age, not (hopefully) the archetypal hag but the archetype of the wise woman and healer. And just as suddenly, I experienced a welcome renaissance of my interest in spirituality and an increasing desire to explore different approaches to healing. During the 30 or so years I had been in medicine, time constraints and the growing reliance on technology inevitably affected the traditional doctor-patient relationship. This was a sadness to me since I felt that, collectively, as allopathic doctors, we had stopped looking at the whole person and were increasingly being forced down a reductionist pathway where there were only specialists in bits of people. The concept of looking at a disease holistically became the new focus of my left brain, and I decided to attend as many complementary and alternative medicine workshops as I could to experience what they had to offer. The zeal with which I had addressed my clinical research had found a new and exciting outlet: I would explore everything from reflexology to kinesiology to see if I could learn anything useful to integrate within allopathic medicine safely. Meantime, the physical changes I was experiencing, particularly in my brain function, were, I suspect, a prerequisite for what happened in the autumn of 2001.

It had been a fairly uneventful day. I'd worked in the female clinic in the morning, then spent a few hours engaged in an admin session in the afternoon, and was in bed by 10 p.m. Then, suddenly, I was rudely awakened at 5 a.m. in the middle of a lucid dream in which one of my male colleagues, Steven, had died. Only I knew it wasn't a dream.

I'd experienced that same absolute knowing only once before when my Latin teacher at school had died. In this dream, which I somehow knew was set six months in the future, I was observing a conversation between two colleagues who were sadly reminiscing about our late friend and discussing his replacement. Instantly, I was fully awake and distraught. Whilst I didn't know much about Steven, who was a family man with young children, he had always struck me as a very nice guy. I got up and drove to work to comfort the staff. It was 6:30 a.m. and only the cleaners were in the building. Since they had never seen me in the department before 8 a.m., they were clearly concerned that something might be wrong. Afraid they would think I was mad if I told them the truth, I lied, saying I had urgent paperwork to do before the clinic opened.

A few hours later, news of Steven's unexpected death came via a phone call. I was upset, but at the same time, I felt a surreal sense of calmness, just as I had done 35 years earlier when I had sensed that my teacher, Mr Sharpe, had died. This tragic event was a watershed in my belief system. Memories of my experiences as a child and as an adult at St. Thomas' came flooding back. But I was also upset because I did not want to have such alarming predictive dreams. Professionally, I was at the height of my career, both academically and clinically. I was chairman of our consultants' committee with all the associated responsibilities and gravitas of the post. Hence, I was acutely aware that I could not afford to appear deluded. And still, I was becoming increasingly obsessed with discovering how I had been able to sense Steven's death. What to do?

Ultimately, my enquiring mindset prevailed, and I decided that since I had no rational explanation for precognition, I would make it my next area of study and explore the mystical underworld further.

I found a medium called Zena, who was both a spiritualist minister and a high priestess in Wicca. And so began my journey of discovery into paranormal phenomena, little knowing that this decision would not only lead to my appointment to the Royal College of Physicians' Integrated Health Committee but also to a memorable and highly amusing meeting with Prince (now King) Charles.

Zena

Zena was a highly recommended spiritual mentor and teacher who lived in a small council house near my Swansea home. She was a close friend and mentor of a GP chum who was also on a spiritual path.

When I booked a reading with Zena, I told her about my paranormal experiences and how my latest dream had upset me. I did not want to have premonitions about bad events over which I had no control. Feeling that an unseen hand was pushing me to develop my abilities as a spiritual healer, Zena advised me to train with the Healer Practitioner Association International (HPAI), where she herself had trained.

The HPAI offered a free two-year course comprising weekly evening sessions. The only costs were a small contribution to hiring a meeting room for the group and our teaching materials. The time commitment was considerable as I was still working full-time at Singleton. Still, I knew I had to pursue this opportunity if I ever wanted to understand why I seemed to see the world through a different lens than my peers.

Fourteen of us started the course, but only three completed it and became registered Spiritual Healers. The first few introductory meetings on spiritual philosophy, health and safety and legal issues were held at Zena's home. We moved to a hired room nearby once we started practising. At first, I found it really difficult to relax. The pervasive scents and sights of incense, candles, spiritual icons, and crystals were out of my comfort zone. Coming straight from a busy day at the hospital, I found it almost impossible to calm my mind. It wasn't until I started reciting a poem about soul friends, which I had written shortly after reading John O'Donohue's book "Anam Cara,"[*] that I finally attained

---

[*] I've included my poem, also titled Anam Cara, in Appendix III.

a different state of consciousness that enabled me to connect to and commune with my Spirit guides. And that's when the weird stuff really started happening.

It began slowly and subtly. Interested colleagues who asked for demonstrations would report feelings of electricity coursing down their arms as my hands hovered over their shoulders. Others would say, "I felt as though you were somehow lifting me right out of my body." Then, as the weeks and months passed and my psychological comfort zone expanded to incorporate more of these strange experiences, I found my academically-trained left brain questioning what was really going on. I had initially explained it to myself as a simple transference of energy. But was that true? How could I know for sure? I longed for the simplicity of the therapeutic gold standard of the double-blind, placebo-controlled studies of my youth. But how can you measure the immeasurable? And how can you channel healing energy without the recipient being aware?

I was on holiday with my mother in Cornwall when I had the perfect opportunity to conduct a single-blinded experiment.

***

One sunny afternoon, we were exploring the countryside around our holiday cottage when we came across a sleepy little village with a log cabin community craft shop. It was near a small river and had shaded parking, which is required when a dog is your travelling companion.

The shop was full of hand-crafted goods from paintings and pottery to crystals and candles. My mother was busy looking for suitable gifts whilst I chatted to the checkout lady, Anne, who looked about ten years older than me and seemed to be distraught. When I enquired whether something was wrong, Anne confided that she had just taken a call from her husband's carer. She felt she needed to be home with her sick husband but was committed to serving at the shop. My instinct was to help somehow, but I thought it inappropriate to blurt out, "I am a doctor and a trainee spiritual healer; may I send you some healing energy?" Plus, my training had emphasized that we should never attempt to channel healing energy to someone who had not first requested it. Even so, it was clear that this woman desperately needed to offload some of her anxiety. As she proceeded to tell me her life history, I knew I had to try and help.

Without breaking eye contact, I placed my palms on either side of Anne's right hand, and silently prayed for healing energy to flow through me into her, but only if it were in her best interests. With Anne's eyes still locked on mine, I stayed like that for several minutes, praying for her to be at peace as she continued sharing her woes. Then suddenly, she abruptly stopped speaking and, with an alarmed expression, raised her right arm and announced, "My arm is very hot, and the heat is travelling to my shoulder. What have you done to me?" Then, just as suddenly, the tension on Anne's face softened, chased away by the appearance of a slow, peaceful smile, and she uttered, "I feel wonderful."

Unaware of what had just transpired and having completed her shopping, Mum came to the counter and made her purchase, after which Anne turned to me, gave me a prolonged hug that spoke volumes, and we departed.

That was the only time I attempted to channel healing without the recipient's permission. But the experience was satisfying evidence that something very real occurs when energy flows between people.

Further evidence came one evening when I went swimming at a local hotel leisure club. On a previous visit, I had spoken to a woman called Elaine, whose daughter had just died from ovarian cancer. Understandably, Elaine was very distressed and downcast. During our conversation,

I shared my belief that our consciousness is eternal and that she would meet up with her daughter again in the afterlife. I hadn't seen Elaine since, but when I arrived at the pool on this occasion, I saw her standing at the shallow end of the pool, talking to a beautifully coiffed lady I had never seen before. When I swam up to them, Elaine introduced me to her friend, Margaret, as "the doctor who is training as a spiritual healer." I was completely unprepared for what came next.

Recoiling as if she had been stung by a bee, Margaret bristled and barked, "You don't believe in all that rubbish, do you?!" Wanting a quiet swim, I chose not to react to her disdain and replied that while the left-brained, academic doctor part of me agreed with her, my intuitive right brain did believe it.

"Show me!" Margaret snorted. Unfazed by her aggressive tone and wanting to get on with my swim, I invited her to hold her right hand out vertically and placed my hands a short distance away on either side. I did not know then if healing vibes could travel through water (I've since learned they can), but I decided to give it a go just so I could get away.

"Just as I thought, nothing!" exclaimed Margaret triumphantly before abruptly ordering me to try her left hand. Bemused by her contradictory attitude, I duly placed my hands on each side of Margaret's left hand. Her reaction was instantaneous. As if tasered, she immediately jerked and fell back into the water, ruining her immaculate hairdo and terrifying herself in the process.

Unable to stifle her laughter, Elaine blurted out, "That'll teach you!" as a shocked Margaret exclaimed, "I felt a bolt of energy go right up my left arm. It lodged in my elbow and forced me backwards into the water." Feeling somewhat vindicated, I slunk off for a swim with Margaret's voice ringing in my ears as she admitted to Elaine, "Well, she certainly couldn't have faked that."

I only saw Margaret once more when I crossed her path in the changing room a month or so later. Her surprise and horror were written all over her face as she immediately scuttled backwards to the corner of the room, muttering, "Don't come near me!" To this day, I have no idea how she ended up in the water with her immaculate hairdo hanging in dripping strands around her shocked face. But I do wonder if some mischievous Spirit guide had decided that Margaret needed a baptism—in more ways than one.

During that period, I occasionally felt conflicted. Having attained my first degree in biology/biophysics with extensive training in scientific methods mainly based on Newtonian physics, I couldn't help wondering if training as a healer might be a waste of time. However, as I soon learned, such thoughts were almost always succeeded by a "spiritual clip on the ear" to get me back on track. One such ear-clipping took place towards the end of my training when we were asked to bring along volunteers for our hands-on energy work.

For the final three months of the course, an external examiner was appointed to observe each of the probationary healers. At that time, I still had to attend occasional academic meetings at the university and one such meeting fell on the same day as my evening spiritual healing session.

Following the committee meeting, as we were mingling over coffee, I was introduced to a very smartly dressed lady called Teresa. Teresa was a senior academic, and we were both enjoying our conversation about our various projects when I realized it was getting late. Reluctantly excusing myself, and without really thinking about what I was saying, I told Teresa I had to go as I had an evening class on spiritual healing to attend. Immediately, Teresa's expression changed to one of baffled amusement. "Why would someone so left-brained as you even contemplate becoming involved in paranormal activities?" she asked. So, I gave her a brief explanation and said I needed a guinea pig for that evening's session. "Would you like to come and see for yourself?" I asked her. To my surprise (and not a little trepidation), Teresa said she would.

When Teresa arrived for our session, still dressed in her working clothes and looking every inch the professional senior academic she was, I immediately sensed her profound discomfort. I couldn't help wondering what had impelled her to step so far out of her comfort zone.

I thanked her for coming and invited her to be seated. Once the session started, I stood behind Teresa with my hands gently positioned over her shoulders. It didn't take long for me to fall into a semi-trance state, and as I tuned into her energy field and connected with Spirit, I felt an overwhelming sense of unconditional love for Teresa. This was followed by the feeling that I was in a totally different place and my consciousness was being taken over by someone who was very fond of Teresa.

I was still very new to spiritual healing, and while becoming accustomed to the different ways in which Spirit can manifest, I presumed that the things I saw and the emotions I felt were just part of my imagination. As a result, I would sometimes casually share the information I gathered. When I described what I had felt and seen, the change in Teresa's affect was profound. She told me I had accurately described the unusual place where a close and much-loved late relative had worked. She was disturbed since she had only lived and taught within Newtonian reality and could not understand how I knew such things. Our brief encounter had caused a state of cognitive dissonance. I suspect she had come to the meeting expecting her view of reality to be reaffirmed, but quite the opposite had happened. I spoke to Teresa a month later, and she was fine, having perhaps come to terms with the experience. I learned to be cautious when interacting with very left-brained folk that day, since some find the bridge between Newtonian and quantum reality a challenging and disturbing one to cross.

In the following chapters, I will describe several paranormal experiences I had over the ensuing decade and how I finally made some sense of it all. These experiences and subsequent explorations of non-orthodox medicine may encourage other healthcare workers to consider a more holistic approach to healing.

CHAPTER 6

The Power of Prayer

Although prayer is an accepted practice in countless world religions, I had never thought about its validity or effectiveness until I intuitively used it when I carried out my research into the efficacy of metronidazole in the treatment of malodorous vaginal discharges. I have already discussed how I used to hold my research patients' notes and pray for them to keep their appointments. The Genito-Urinary Medicine clinic at St. Thomas' Hospital was hardly an overtly sacred place. But I believe the location is less important when your intentions are good and your mind passionately focuses on an outcome. However, after training as a spiritual healer, synchronicities, coincidences, and the answering of prayers became more frequent and more than a little spooky.

One morning in 2004, I received a phone call from a respected local GP who wanted some advice about chlamydia treatment for one of his patients. When he asked how I was, I told him I was training as a spiritual healer, adding that I wouldn't blame him for laughing since I was still known as an academic, research-orientated doctor. It was a gamekeeper turned poacher scenario. "On the contrary," he replied before sharing that he had recently seen a woman who had presented six months earlier with a massive fungating breast tumour. "She was referred for emergency treatment but had never attended," he added. "Yet her breast was normal when she recently showed up in my clinic. She said she had prayed the tumour away."

Whether this patient actually had breast cancer was unknown, but my colleague was sufficiently impressed to not deride my pursuit of non-orthodox treatment. The following stories are just a few examples of my spooky experiences involving prayers.

A Patient's Prayer: The Survivor of Childhood Sexual Abuse

In 2005, I was in the middle of my spiritual healing training and paranormal experiences were becoming part of my everyday life at work. I had developed what I sensed was a link with Archangel Michael and it was to him I prayed when doing my hands-on healing. His presence was often signalled by a feeling of electricity running down my spine to my left foot and the hairs on my neck standing on end.

A bright young woman in her early 20s came to see me one morning. It was her first visit, and as I asked her routine questions, I suddenly noticed a feeling of pins and needles in my neck and an inner voice said, "She was sexually abused as a child." Without pausing, I blurted out the words, "You were sexually abused as a child, weren't you?" (I hasten to add that neither before nor since have I ever said this to a patient.) The patient burst into tears and got up and hugged me, saying she had seen her GP a few days before and had told him about the abuse but felt he had not believed her because she was a late discloser. As a result, she was contemplating suicide and had been praying for someone to believe her. I told her that once a month, we had a psychosexual therapy clinic and that, fortuitously, the psychosexual therapist was there that morning and would have a cancellation.

"How do you know there will be a cancellation?" she asked.

"Because I would not have been told you were abused if there wasn't a vacancy," I explained.

When I popped over to the other side of the clinic to arrange for my patient to be seen, I found our lovely psychotherapist, Noeleen, hovering in the corridor. Noeleen had just been told her 10 a.m. patient had cancelled, and she had an hour to fill. I explained what had happened, and my patient was seen immediately. Her prayers had indeed been answered.

What amazes me is that whenever paranormal things happened, my patients (and colleagues) seldom blinked an eyelid. One would expect at least occasional expressions of disbelief, but that never happened.

An Angelic Invitation to Edinburgh

In 2003, I had a bizarre experience which I can only describe as being "zapped" with what I was later told was "blue star energy." Whilst I appeared to function normally, I felt inwardly dissociated, depressed, and as if my energy field was way out of synchrony with my body. According to shamanic belief, these symptoms may be due to soul loss. I scheduled a Korotkov beogram (the image formed during Gas Discharge Visualisation GDV) session in London to find out what was going on. The therapist said my results showed that my chakras* were mainly outside my physical body. This frame of mind persisted, and by late

---

* "Chakra" is a Sanskrit word meaning "wheel." It refers to energy points within the body that comprise spinning vortices of energy that apparently connect the physical body to the energy body. For a more detailed description, see *Wheels of Life: A User's Guide to the Chakra System* by Anodea Judith.

summer/autumn of 2006, I wondered if I would ever feel truly normal again. I thought about talking to my GP, Bethan, but couldn't quite get my head around the envisaged conversation:

Bethan: "What can I do for you, Anona?"

Anona: "Well, Bethan, I have a problem… I am suffering from soul loss, and my chakras are out of balance."

I could imagine the expression on her face.

Regular doctors don't have a cure for soul loss or poorly balanced chakras. I should know I am a regular doctor.

So there I was, depressed, bereft of vitality, doubting my inner reality, afraid I would remain in this state for the rest of my life, and yet acutely aware that drugs would be poison. I had to find my own cure, and I prayed for divine intervention.

Then, late one summer evening in 2006, everything started to change.

I had been working at home for about ten hours and, tired and hungry, decided a stir fry would be the quickest meal. Mum and Keston, my Jack Russell terrier, were back in Abergavenny, and I had the place to myself. I was tossing the vegetables when I suddenly became aware of what I can only describe as an angelic presence in the kitchen, who claimed to be Archangel Michael. He told me to attend a specific workshop in Edinburgh in November saying, "You will find someone there who will give you back your soul and heal you."

My first thought was, "Nonsense, Michael. You are just my subconscious mind tormenting me. And even if you are who you claim to be, there is no way I will spend thousands on a workshop in Edinburgh in winter, with no rational reason for going and no friends to accompany me."

Still, the voice persisted: "You must go to Edinburgh. You WILL find someone who will heal you."

"Yeah, yeah," I responded. "But I have already attended similar workshops, and I don't want to repeat them for no good reason."

Still, the inner voice kept insisting… "You must go to Edinburgh. You will meet someone who will heal you. You must go to Edinburgh…" over and over as time stood still and my stir fry passed beyond edible.

Fed up with arguing with this discarnate being, I eventually gave in. "Okay. Okay." I said. "I'm hungry and tired, so you win. I will phone the organiser tomorrow."

The next day I phoned the workshop co-ordinator and spoke to a woman who asked me what had led me to book this specific course which was divided into two topics. I felt it was probably a bad idea to say the absolute truth—i.e. that Archangel Michael had popped into my kitchen for a chat and told me to book the workshop because I would meet someone who would retrieve my soul. She might just think I was crazy.

I was taking a significant risk since the trip put my inner belief system and possibly my ability to work on the line. I was raised in relative poverty, so I greatly respect money. £4000 was a lot to spend on an invisible angel's whim, but I had no choice; life without my soul was grim since I had no spiritual self-esteem and I felt like the walking dead. I told her I was a doctor, and we chatted briefly about my interest in the workshops. I also promised myself that if I did not meet someone who would help me, I would consider myself delusional, resign from my job, and see a psychiatrist when I got home.

The journey started with a taxi ride to Cardiff Airport, then a flight to Edinburgh and another taxi to my B&B. I stayed in a guesthouse run by a charming French lady I had met on a course in London the year before.

The following day dawned cold, wet, and gloomy. *A good match for my mood*, I thought as I took a taxi to the venue, where I stood in the registration line, eyeing up the eclectic mix of archetypes from computer nerds to weekend Reiki Masters, and idly wondering if they have Reiki Mistresses. Overall, they seemed like a friendly bunch of folk. Still, wherever I scanned, I couldn't see anyone holding up an airport-style placard with the words, "Archangel Michael's emissary seeks person whose soul needs retrieval." I didn't know what I had been expecting, but it was little more than blind faith that had brought me so far from my home and so far outside my comfort zone.

The course leader was engaging, but as the days passed without finding anyone I could bond with, I was feeling increasingly isolated.

Edinburgh is a beautiful city, but I had no soul, and it was beginning to seem like I had lost my mind, too. Every morning, I walked the mile or so to the venue alone. The weather remained chilly, and the largely uphill trek was tiring. I could afford a taxi, but I was cross with myself for being such an idiot as to think that Archangel Michael had actually communicated with me, so the walk was a self-imposed penance; my sackcloth and ashes—a physical pain to balance the guilt I felt for wasting so much money and energy on an apparent fantasy. Many may think that even believing in angels is delusional, so I was really pushing the boundaries of my belief system. Old-school-trained, I would have resigned rather than let my patients be at risk from a deluded doctor.

By day five, there was still no sign of my knight in shining armour. I was doubly gutted. First, it seemed no one would bring my power back to me, and second, I had wasted a lot of money on what must have been a daydream. *Was this the end of my spiritual quest?*

My morale remained low. A close friend phoned most evenings, but otherwise, I was cut off from my ordinary reality. Finally, the first of the two workshops was over, and there was a day's break before the more advanced course started.

Thankfully, everything began to change when many of the attendees at the first workshop left and a new influx of people joined us. It was a smaller group of perhaps 100, and many were like-minded, spiritually-aware folk so I felt less lonely.

The first day involved deep meditation work in a semi-darkened hall. One of the first to emerge from the relative darkness, I headed towards the more brightly lit coffee room, initially unaware that I was rubbing the centre of my forehead rather than my actual eyes. I chuckled as I realised I was rubbing my third eye, which the meditation must have opened.

The afternoon event was focused on demonstrating how to exchange bits of one's consciousness with another person. It was similar to a mind-melding technique I had learned at one of the late Bill Harrison's workshops a few years prior. We divided into small groups of four and were asked to choose a partner with skills we would like to acquire. Then, using focused attention, we were encouraged to send the knowledge to the other person.

My mind was torn. *What a load of nonsense*, my left brain tersely chimed in, as my less judgemental, more relaxed right brain thought *I might as well give it a go*. Ever the practical punter bouncing between the world of thought and the "real world," I announced that I was a good teacher and could make delicious mint sauce.

"Well, I'm very good at housework, and I would like to meld minds for your mint sauce recipe," announced the chap to my right brightly.

Since I had absolutely no interest in improving my housework skills, I opted to pair up with the woman opposite me, whose gift—the ability to talk with angels—was more appealing.

After several minutes of earnestly trying to send the energy of our gifts to each other and not having felt anything, I had to confess that the experience had been a failure for me. But, apparently, the same was not true for my partner, who emerged from her trance with a serious expression, looked me straight in the eye and declared, "I must talk to you when this session is over. I have been able to speak to angels since I was a small child, and I must tell you that Archangel Michael is around you," she went on to explain in a tone of absolute knowing and determination. "In fact, the only reason I came here was because Michael told me there would be someone here that I must heal. *You are that person.*"

Given my gamble in coming to Edinburgh, my response was low-key. "Good. I've been looking for you all week!" I said as if we were two old friends who had just made a date for coffee. As surreal as it was, neither of us seemed surprised at this sudden coalescing of our inner and outer realities.

My proverbial "knight" had turned out to be a woman named Sharon. Later that day, we sat in a corner of the coffee room and shared details of the events that had brought us together. I learned that Sharon, who was married and did not live in mainland Britain, had left her family and travelled a long way to follow Archangel Michael's edict.

Sharon told me that something had caused part of my soul to splinter off and leave me. Now it was time to bring it back. As prosaically as if I was a patient sitting in a dentist's chair, having a crown replaced, Sharon worked on me by placing one hand on my head and the other hovering over my heart chakra. I felt a gentle heat moving through my body as, channelling Archangel Michael's thoughts, Sharon spoke out loud. "I am so sorry. It was meant to happen, but I took my eye off the ball, and you were not meant to be so badly hurt."

It was all over in less than two minutes. I thanked Sharon and said goodbye, fully knowing I was finally healed in every fibre of my being. A repeat beogram confirmed it. My chakras were now fully aligned again, and my power, my life force energy—call it what you will—was once again firing on all cylinders. For the first time in several years, I felt truly at peace.

That was the last time I saw Sharon. But it was proof to my sometimes sceptical, medically-trained left brain that angels may help us and that Sharon might well be what many refer to as an Earth Angel. I am very grateful for her brief presence in my life.

A Workshop With Lynne McTaggart

On March 11th, 2007, I was one of 400 like-minded folks who attended Lynne McTaggart's two-day "Intention Experiment" workshop at Imperial College in London.

The author of several NY Times best-selling books, including *The Field: The Quest for the Secret Force of the Universe*, Lynne McTaggart is an award-winning journalist who first shook the British medical establishment with the success of her monthly "What Doctors Don't Tell You" newsletter. Now one of several widely-respected voices from science, medicine, and the media working in the New Thought/Consciousness studies arena, she has greatly influenced my approach to understanding the science of the "paranormal" and the existential need for modern medicine to embrace at least some holistic/Green Medicine concepts.

As anticipated, it was a truly magical weekend. The weather was blissfully sunny, and having met up with my old friend Shireen, I was looking forward to a mini adventure.

The workshop ended with a ten-minute prayer, during which all 400 participants gazed at a screen projection of two geranium leaves placed in a super-cooled chamber some 5,000 miles away in Arizona.

Our instructions were to pray that one of the leaves, selected by tossing a coin, would emit more biophotons than its chum. Shireen and I were conflicted. We were both trained in spiritual healing, so this task felt like sending a death wish to the selected leaf. Of course, such concerns seemed madness since it was only a leaf, and the concept that we could influence events 5000 miles away with our thoughts was enough to override our reservations.

All too soon, the ten minutes had passed, and the workshop was over. Lynne said she would email us the results in about six weeks. In fact, it was only a few days later when I received an email saying that the selected leaf had glowed so much it could be seen by the naked eye. I phoned Shireen, and we both wept, sad for the leaf that had lost its life for the experiment and joyful that the experiment had worked and that what shamans have been telling us for millennia was true—plants have a form of consciousness.

The following weekend, I attended another workshop led by a medium who had given me a reading a year earlier in a session that should have been 20 minutes but continued beyond an hour. We spent our lunch break catching up on each other's news. When she confided her desire to verify her psychic talents scientifically, I said I'd be happy to see if anyone at Swansea University could do the necessary tests. It seemed like such a small thing to offer—just one friend offering a hand of support to another. Little did I know that in extending this offer, I was setting off a chain of remarkable events that would provide all the evidence I could want of the extraordinary power of thought, intention, and prayers.

When I shared my medium friend's ambition with Shireen later that evening, Shireen suggested that if we could arrange some tests for the medium, we could film them for an independent documentary to raise funds for consciousness research. *Good idea*, I thought, as I duly passed the message on. Two days later, on March 20th, 2007, I boarded the 9:30 a.m. train from Swansea to London to attend a meeting of the Royal College of Physicians' Integrated Health Committee (IHC), to which I was appointed the year before.

As I opened my book by the American physician Dr Larry Dossey—who is a huge proponent of the validity and importance of prayer, spirituality, and other non-physical factors in healing—geranium leaves, and my medium friend's aspiration to validate her gift were, unsurprisingly, very much on my mind.

Finding a team to incarnate this research project would be a challenge. Whilst I felt confident that I might find someone among my professional colleagues who could set up and conduct the tests, I had no idea where I would find a documentary filmmaker. The nearest I had ever come to that particular arena was when I had helped with a BBC 2 documentary on chlamydia ten years prior.

With one portion of my mind loosely focused on Larry Dossey's book and the rest slowly lulled by the sounds and rhythm of the train's wheels into an altered state of consciousness, I decided I would pray for the appearance of a documentary filmmaker.

Since Lynne McTaggart's teachings about "powering up" were fresh in my mind, I decided to mentally recite my special "Anam Cara" poem to help slow down my brainwave patterns and move deeper into the alpha state of wakeful relaxation.

I sat alone at a table for four in an almost empty carriage when a woman joined the train at the next stop and sat diagonally opposite me. As I politely acknowledged her presence, I was startled by an unexpected wave of energy pushing me into the back of my seat. I immediately recalled what the medical intuitive, mystic, and author Caroline Myss had once said at one of her workshops about such occurrences being the soul's response to someone who is part of your soul's journey crossing your path. Clearly, it was time to stop daydreaming and start paying attention. The journey continued in silence for a few more minutes until, with a nod towards Larry Dossey's book, my fellow passenger asked where I came from.

I chuckled and said, "Well, I'm not sure . . . it's either Atlantis or Sirius."

We chatted for about twenty minutes or so about my work with the IHC, in which she seemed keenly interested. Then, aware that other passengers might not be so interested in quantum physics and how it related to medical thinking, we fell into a natural silence. At Paddington, we shook hands and were just on the verge of saying goodbye when, baffled by the initial energy surge and wondering how Caroline Myss could have got it so wrong, I impulsively decided that this stranger should not pass out of my life without my at least finding something to explain the energy surge. "What do you do for a living?" I asked.

"I'm an independent documentary filmmaker," she replied.

My jaw dropped. Then, emboldened by the synchronicity, I told her of my prayer. Amazed by the seeming coincidence, she handed me her card. Her name was Deborah Kingsland, and she was about to leave for Australia, where she would be covering a Complementary and Alternative Medicine (CAM) meeting!

I took a taxi to the Royal College of Physicians in Regents Park and, as usual, felt awed by the building's ambience and the sight of paintings of eminent, if mainly long-dead, practitioners of our craft peering down at me in apparent muted curiosity.

I was seated next to Professor George Lewith, a professor of Complementary Medicine at Southampton University. George was an affable, avuncular man who, fortuitously, had been a fellow student at Westminster Medical School in the 1970s. Naturally, I followed up on my conversation with Deborah, who had said her group would be happy to discuss my project if I could find someone to do the tests. Sadly, our desire to research this area of consciousness did not yield any results, although I did learn a formidable lesson in the power of prayer.

My presence on the Integrated Health Committee and links with Professor Lewith influenced my decision to mentor a young medical student, Natalie Taylor, now Major Taylor RAMC. In 2007, she and I undertook a research project into the needs of our local medical student population about familiarisation with complementary and alternative medicine. Following the publication of our findings in 2008, we were invited to join a group of doctors and medical students in Kerala, where we studied Ayurvedic medicine under the auspices of Prince Charles' Foundation for Integrated Health, which, in turn, led to an unexpected but very memorable meeting with the King himself.

CHAPTER 7

Meeting the King

It was July 1st, 2008, and I had travelled to London to meet with the group of medical colleagues with whom I had travelled to Kerala. We were meeting our group leader at the Royal Liberal Club in Horse Guard's Parade at 2 p.m. for a brief workshop, followed by a lecture on security arrangements, bag checks, and a briefing on royal etiquette and the proper protocol for being introduced to and interacting with HRH before being escorted over to Clarence House.

After our invitations and identity documents were scrutinised, we were advised to be on our best behaviour and to address the Prince in the first instance as "Your Royal Highness" and follow it up with a bow or curtsey. After that, we could address him as Sir. My Welsh working-class and somewhat lukewarm republican upbringing made me feel uneasy at having to be so deferential. But I was curious to meet this seemingly atypical member of the Royal Family, so I was happy to comply. However, the dos and don'ts, shalts and shalt nots of the protocol were repeated so frequently that by the time we left for Clarence House, my head was aching from my continuous memory-mantra of… "Your Royal Highness, then Sir… Your Royal Highness, then Sir…"

It didn't help that the march from Horse Guards Parade was a long one, and I was wearing both a new suit and new shoes that were quite unsuitable for walking far, especially in the heat. By the time we reached Clarence House, my feet were covered in massive blisters, and I could barely walk. I just hoped my mantra would be sufficient to hard-wire the words into my brain.

On arrival at Clarence House, we were ushered into a large reception room. My attention was temporarily diverted from my painfully blistered feet by the sight of dozens of valuable objects d'art on display and a sea of gloriously ornate Persian carpets covering the floor. The paintings on the wall were stunning, and everywhere I looked, I spotted little items of family memorabilia. I vividly remember being captivated by a painting of the Queen Mother. But the diversion didn't last long. I longed to take my shoes off and sit down, but, strangely, there were no chairs, sofas, or chaise longues in sight.

We were divided into groups of four to six people. Since most of the Kerala group were General Practitioners interested in Alternative Medicine, and I was the sole consultant present, I was allotted three medical students. We were offered tea, not in fine porcelain china, but in attractive cups that were clearly designed to last, and decorated with an image of Clarence House gardens. As we sipped our tea, we pretended to engage in small talk and not be too obvious in our darting glances at the main entrance.

Eventually, Prince Charles arrived accompanied by a personal assistant and what I took to be a bodyguard. Suddenly, the atmosphere in the room was electric. Several security men, each with the energy and lure of James Bond, scanned the room. The comedic side of my personality desperately wanted to mimic the famous Mae West quote: "Is that a gun in your pocket, or are you just pleased to see me?!" But I resisted. One look at HRH, and I forgot all about my blistered feet.

We were the second group to be presented to HRH. His energy field was overwhelming, and, his voice's deep, smooth timbre conjured up images of ripe plums steeped in maple syrup. And just like that, I was smitten. HRH was no longer the future King; he was just a man and the energetic equal of my fantasy list of ideal men Bill Clinton (but only whilst he was president), Sean Bean (wearing his major Sharpe outfit) and Mel Gibson (as he appeared in Braveheart) all in one. How would I cope!

Finally, it was our turn to be introduced to HRH. I managed to say, "Pleased to meet you, your Royal Highness," as etiquette demanded. Then the prince asked, "So how did a Genitourinary physician become a spiritual healer?" And suddenly my cup rattled on its saucer and my entire body started trembling. I couldn't seem to control it. It had all happened so suddenly I was at a loss to know what to do.

"Not to worry," HRH kindly uttered in a voice that would heal the soul. "I have that effect on a lot of people." My heart melted. Bill Clinton, Sean Bean, Mel Gibson—eat your heart out! This is one genuinely gentle man. Then, to my horror, I blurted out, "Oh, it's not you, Sir. It's just that we have spent an hour being told to call you Sir. And the only men I call Sir are those I am about to examine. I am terrified you may cough and I might react inappropriately."

Fortunately, the prince roared with laughter. But still, the cup continued to rattle. So, in the hope that it might reduce my fear, I tentatively asked HRH if I could hold his hand to relieve my anxiety. "Of course," he said, offering me his right hand. It was a large hand, more like that of a farmer than I had expected. I was comforted, and within moments, my trembling ceased. But I was enjoying the contact so much that I cheekily asked if I could tune into his aura. He seemed bemused, but invited me to carry on. So I did.

To my surprise, my mind's eye immediately saw a Merlin-like figure holding a staff standing behind and slightly to the right of HRH. I was then shown an image of HRH's heart chakra. My respect deepened as I felt his enormous wisdom and compassion. I did not tell him all I had sensed but said, "You have Merlin energy around you, and you have a large heart chakra." When he asked what I meant about his heart chakra, I said, "It means you are a very caring and compassionate person, Sir."

Several seconds of somewhat pregnant silence passed before I suddenly realised that my jacket had popped open and the price tag that I had forgotten to remove was on full display. Laughing, I grabbed the tag and said, "I hope you appreciate this, Sir. You are the only man I have tarted up for in 30 years!" Given my somewhat ample figure and woeful lack of dress sense, I wasn't surprised when our group erupted into fits of laughter.

What happened next was one of the most mischievous episodes of my life. Still curious about how an academic doctor had become a spiritual healer, HRH encouraged me to continue. So I reeled off a potted life history, followed by a few tales of how patients were sometimes accompanied by the spirits of dead relatives who often helped with their diagnosis and healing. I then rounded it off by telling him that someone had even arrived with the Spirit of a pet horse in tow. HRH listened intently, as if trying to assess my sanity, and then, in a very respectful but amused tone said, "Dr Blackwell, do tell me, don't your colleagues think you are rather mad?"

Looking him straight in the eyes, I said with the utmost gravitas, "Well, Sir, I have a degree in biophysics and medicine, a Diploma in Theology, am an FRCP, and have published dozens of research papers including three Lancet papers, two of which helped permanently alter clinical practice in the UK. I have a distinction award, was Chair of our Trust's Consultants Committee, teach regularly in our medical school, and have given numerous international presentations for over 25 years. I am also a member of the Royal College of Physicians Integrated Health Committee, so, Sir, if I mention to a colleague that a patient came to see me accompanied by a Spirit pet, they usually ask me what type of pet. Sir." I think he got the point.

Fortunately, an aide indicated that our allotted time with HRH was coming to an end. Everyone was getting ready to leave when, to my surprise, Prince Charles came over to me, grabbed my right hand and asked if I was still afraid of him.

Determined to be on my best behaviour, I said, "No, I am okay now, thank you, Sir."

HRH released my hand and turned to walk away, then glanced back and said, "You never told me what Merlin energy is?" I should have just smiled politely and left it there. But, of course, I didn't.

HRH was just four metres away. Still reeling from the unexpected hand-holding, all presence of mind deserted me. I gave the Prince a look that started at his feet and rose slowly upward to his eyes, and with a cheeky wink, softly asked, "Do you really want to know, Babe?" As the full force of what I'd inferred hit me, I started stumbling out an apology, "I am so sorry, babe—Sir," I spluttered. "I don't want to be locked up in the tower," before quickly trying to cover my clumsy gaffe with an explanation of how, as the Prince of Wales and Britain's future King, he might naturally attract archetypal mythical Merlin energy to him.

To my relief, Prince Charles seemed to find my gaffe hilarious, so I asked if a picture could be taken with him for our Trust's Good News page.

As we were leaving Clarence House, one of HRH's aides came up to me to say that the Prince was pleased to meet me and hoped I would continue with my work. I like to think it was his gracious way of telling me not to worry about my lack of formality. It certainly confirmed that we were indeed fortunate to have such a thoughtful and wise heir apparent.

As a sweet footnote, I met Prince Charles again at a meeting at the King's Fund a year or so later. It was a brief, handshaking encounter. He chuckled as we shook hands, so I am sure he remembered me.

A day to remember, indeed!

PART 3

FOLLOWING THE
YELLOW BRICK ROAD

CHAPTER 8

The Boy Who Walked Through the Wall and Other True Stories

The Boy Who Walked Through the Wall
* * *

It was an exceptionally busy Thursday morning female clinic, and the waiting room was full. I knew it would be a long haul, possibly four-and-a-half-hour clinic, and I mentally girded my loins to face my patients. "It's going to be busy today," a nurse said, which we both knew meant *Get a move on and no messing about with holistic healing*. I got the message loud and clear, and we managed to see at least five women in the first hour. I was focused on orthodox medicine, and since I had no students sitting in, there were no delays.

This conventional approach to medical care changed abruptly when a patient came into my room, followed by a boy with the angelic face of a child and the gangly legs of a lad on the edge of puberty. He had curly black hair, wore a white T-shirt and dark shorts, and as he scampered past his mum, he disappeared into the wall behind her. I was not overly surprised at the vision. However, whilst I had become used to my excursions into non-ordinary reality, I lacked the courage to tell the patient for fear of upsetting her. As I continued asking routine questions about past gynaecological and obstetric history, I noted that my patient's demeanour suddenly became profoundly sad. She revealed that she'd had a son who had died young in a tragic accident and had just come from seeing a medium who had told her that his Spirit still followed her everywhere. Reluctant to add to her distress and concerned for my reputation, to my shame, I said nothing.

In light of what I've experienced since, I now believe that the lady—whom it transpired had no medical reason to see me—had been sent by a higher power to have the medium's message confirmed by a white-coated doctor whose word might perhaps carry more credibility and comfort. To this day, I regret my hesitation. From then on, whenever I saw a patient who had no real medical reason to see me, I took it as a red flag that their underlying problem might be more spiritual than physical.

I did not have to wait long before another lady came in accompanied by the Spirit of a teenage boy dressed in school uniform, who I suspected had also died tragically. Since this mother had no apparent need for my medical services either, I took the opportunity to gently share what I was seeing. On this occasion, the woman was totally aware of her son's presence and confirmed that his passing had been a heartbreaking accident. We briefly shared our views about the afterlife, and before leaving, she thanked me for the comfort my words had given her.

Another Mother and Her Spirit Son

Life became more challenging as I combined my spiritual healing training with my heavy orthodox medical practice, whilst also taking care of an increasingly demanding aging mother and ailing uncle. Whenever the stress became too much, I would book a few days break at a health spa in Somerset. I had stayed at this spa many times before, so I knew it to be a serene place with wonderfully attentive staff, delectable food, and accommodation that oozed spiritually healing vibes.

On one occasion, I slept alone in a large bedroom where every shadow seemed ominous. Sleep was elusive, but eventually, I must have nodded off because I suddenly awoke with a start to the sound and sensation of a loud thump, as if someone had jumped from the other side of reality and landed right next to my bed. Instantly wide awake and frightened to put the light on, I cowered under the duvet until sleep eventually claimed me again. The following day, I could not wait to tell the waitress who served breakfast about the paranormal presence I had experienced in my room. But she beat me to it.

"Did you feel the earthquake that hit this area during the night?" she asked excitedly. So much for jumping ghosts!

Aside from that slightly disturbing occurrence, my memories of that spa are all of grace and healing, invariably involving delightful sessions of some form of therapy, including reflexology, and hot stone and Indian head massages. Apart from the young, mainly female groups of jovial day visitors, many of the residents seemed to have come for the healing of their physical and/or mental health issues.

After dinner one evening, I met two women who looked to be somewhere in their 40s enjoying coffee in the drawing room. I sat opposite them, satiated and relaxed in an armchair so soft it felt like a warm cuddle.

But I couldn't help noticing two disturbing things. The first was that one of the women looked extremely downcast and depressed and was clearly being comforted by her companion. The second thing was the Spirit of a wiry young man with light brown curly hair standing behind them.

"Can you tell my mum I'm sorry for what I did, and I want her to forgive me so I can move on?" He asked anxiously, indicating the woman sitting in front of him.

Sensing this was not the best moment to pass on the message, I decided to leave it until the following day and discreetly withdrew. The next morning, I approached the woman who had been doing the comforting and struck up a conversation. She introduced herself as Margery and confided that her cousin, Mary, who was still in bed, had recently lost her son. Taking that as an auspicious opening, I felt able to tell Margery what I had seen and been told by Mary's son. Later that day, Margery approached me asking if I would counsel Mary, who had been very depressed following her son's death. During my private meeting with Mary, she told me of the tragic circumstances in which she'd lost her boy. When I told her that I had seen him and that he wanted me to pass on a message to her, she seemed overwhelmed with relief and gratitude, hugging me in the process.

Margery and Mary left the next day, but before they went, Margery sought me out to say that Mary felt so much more peaceful now she knew that her son was still around and did not want her to grieve for him any longer.

A Three-Way Conversation With Spirit

Sometimes, as with the cockney lady I saw at St. Thomas' Hospital, the people I met were very aware of the presence of their late relatives. On one occasion, while working in a vulval clinic in Swansea, I even had a three-way conversation, speaking verbally with my patient and telepathically with her late husband whilst the patient was also communicating telepathically with him.

Edith was a delightful widow in her late seventies who presented with a simple skin condition. As she tottered into my room, I felt a strong male presence behind her. I was seated at my desk, facing Edith, and standing in the doorway was a man wearing a long dark grey mackintosh and a trilby hat. Though his arms were folded and his gaze was gently focused on Edith, I sensed that this man would not be happy if I said anything that might upset his wife.

After telepathically reassuring him, I asked Edith some routine questions about her gynaecological history and current problem. She told me that her marriage had been consensually platonic and that her late husband had been wheelchair-bound since before they met so she could not have any infection. Edith added that many years previously she'd had a hysterectomy for fibroids.

"When was that?" I enquired.

"Oh, dear, I can't remember. I'll just ask my husband; he's standing right there," she said, pointing to the door. Inwardly pleased that Edith had confirmed what I was seeing, I was nonetheless aware of the fine line between sensing Spirit energy and overt psychosis and thus had to be careful in my response.

"Yes, I see him too," I reassured Edith. "But given he was in a wheelchair all his adult life, why is he standing and looking so well?"

"Because as soon as he died, he was healthy again," Edith explained matter of factly.

What a lovely oxymoronic concept, I thought as I ruminated on my past experience and realised that all the "dead" folk I had encountered had appeared to be perfectly fit with no apparent trace of disease. And all had been fully clothed, just as they had been in life.

"Do you think she is psychotic?" my nurse enquired after Edith and her departed husband had left together, tacitly confirming my suspicion that Edith had been openly chatting about her late husband's presence with other staff members before our appointment.

"I do hope not, because I saw him, too," I responded. "He was wearing a long raincoat and a trilby hat." Given the shocked expression on my nurse's face, I couldn't help thinking it was just as well that Edith had seen me rather than one of my colleagues. She may well have faced an unpleasant and unnecessary psychiatric intervention.

As a footnote to Edith's husband's healthy appearance, my friend Dr Penny Sartori, whom I first met when she attended one of my lectures as a student nurse, is now an internationally recognised researcher in near-death studies. An ICU nurse for seventeen years, Penny has cared for many patients close to death. As a result of her experiences, she began researching near-death experiences (NDEs), which culminated in a PhD and the publication of her monograph "The Near-Death Experiences of Hospitalized Intensive Care Patients: A Five Year Clinical Study"[*] published in 2008, as well as three successful books on this subject.

Dr Sartori tells of one patient with a lifelong fixed deformity of his hand who, following an NDE, became partially healed. Did he die and, like Edith's husband, receive a perfect energy template again, which

---

[*] http://www.drpennysartori.com

manifested as a cure when he was revived? Of course, that is something that we may never know.

A Mother's Love Never Dies

The last patient on my morning list had been booked in as an emergency on the advice of the police following an alleged drug rape. Mary was in her late forties and had a stable, happy marriage with two teenage daughters. She rarely socialized but had recently attended a colleague's bachelorette party and had woken up in a hotel bedroom the following morning, having had her drink spiked. I felt very sorry for Mary since she was clearly distraught. When I checked her details, she suddenly burst into uncontrollable sobs, crying out, "I wish my mother was with me." Within an instant, I became aware of an apparition to my right that appeared like an avenging angel and then felt another consciousness overshadowing me. Somehow, I knew it was Mary's mother.

"I am sure she is with you, Mary," I said. Then, without knowing how I knew, I said, "She died of breast cancer, didn't she?"

"How did you know about my mum's cancer?" Mary gasped, her sobs forgotten. Unsure what to say for fear the truth might make her feel even worse, I waffled on about breast cancer being a common cause of death. Mary looked at me suspiciously, but luckily, my lovely nurse Pam came in to help me get Mary onto the examination couch. As I was about to pass a vaginal speculum to take the necessary swabs, Mary asked Pam if I was psychic. Of course, Pam knew that I was, but she side-stepped the question by asking how old Mary's mother was when she died.

"64," Mary said.

"No," I said, aware that her mother was now hovering above my right shoulder. "She was 65."

"No," Mary repeated, sounding annoyed. "She was my mother, and I know she was 64."

"I don't care who she was; she was 65 when she died," I said confidently, knowing that her mother had been speaking through me.

"Come, come, ladies, don't argue," Pam intervened before asking Mary for her mother's birthdate and the date she had died.

I was correct. Mary had miscalculated. I continued the tests in silence. When we had finished, Mary rose from the couch, half-naked, and embraced me before dressing. I then confided that I was a spiritual healer and believed her mum was actually with her at that moment. Since it was the end of the clinic, I offered Mary some energy healing, gently laying my hands on her shoulders for a few minutes. "Do you have any children?" she asked when the brief session ended.

"No," I replied.

"You have now," she pronounced as she hugged me tightly.

Later that day, Pam confided that Mary had told her that she had entered the clinic surrounded by darkness and had left surrounded by light.

I felt blessed.

Elsie's Aunt

Some years later, another lady came to my clinic. Elsie lived some considerable distance away, and it had taken several hours and three buses for her to get to the clinic. An archetypal Welsh grandmother in her late 50s, Elsie had been happily married for several decades with no other sexual partner than her husband before or after her marriage. She also had no genital tract symptoms, which was a puzzle, given that it was a VD clinic.

When I asked Elsie why she had come to see me, she looked me straight in the eyes and confessed that she honestly didn't know why she had made the appointment.

"Did you specifically ask for me?"

"No," she said. "I just asked for the next available appointment. I have no idea why they booked me into this clinic."

"Do you suspect that your husband might have been unfaithful?" I probed.

Elsie burst into laughter. "Of course not," she chuckled as if I'd told her the funniest joke.

Hmm, I thought, pondering whether Elsie might have some psychiatric condition characterized by a strange need to get a sexually transmitted infection screening. I considered the situation as we sat gazing at each other for several long moments. I felt bad that Elsie had travelled so far for nothing. But how could I help someone who had no symptoms, no risk factors, and clearly did not want or warrant screening?

Then I had an inspiration. Could Elsie's problem be a spiritual issue rather than a physical one? But before I could even express the thought, Elsie's face suddenly became animated as she blurted out with great force, "I know who you are!" My initial alarm that I might have somehow harmed Elsie in the past without knowing it quickly dissipated when she announced, "You have had your hair cut and dyed it blonde."

"Yes," I agreed. "But it's been like this for two years."

"We met at an open circle at a spiritual sanctuary in the Swansea valley a couple of years ago. You gave me a message from my late aunt," Elsie said with a satisfied "that explains everything" smile.

I did not recognize Elsie, but I remembered the circle meeting she referred to. One summer evening, I had travelled with my medium chum

Gill to an open circle near Abercrave, about an hour's drive from my home. It was one of the first open circles I had attended. About 60 people were present, along with a medium giving messages from their departed loved ones. Towards the end of the meeting, the medium asked if anyone in the audience had a message for someone in the circle. I whispered to Gill that I had a message for a lady opposite us, but, as a rookie, I was afraid it might be my imagination. Of course, Gill lost no time outing me, and to my horror, I was soon the centre of the group's attention.

I said I had a female Spirit with me who had just passed from breast cancer, but I was confused because the energy of the Spirit I was communicating with felt like "mother energy," but the message was that the lady should take more care of herself and not totally devote herself to her mother. I thought it must be nonsense until the lady burst into tears, ran over to hug me, and tearfully announced that her aunt had indeed just died of breast cancer. The lady's last words to her aunt were, "You are more like a mother to me than my real mother."

What I find intriguing is how Elsie found me. I had never seen her since then. We had not exchanged names or addresses. Apart from Gill, no one at that meeting knew my identity, and I had no involvement in scheduling patients' appointments. Could Elsie's Spirit guide have had something to do with bringing us together? Had my previous contact with her somehow entangled our consciousness, linking us like some cosmic internet? Indeed, her problem did turn out to be a spiritual one. I have no rational explanation, and can only relate what happened for greater minds to figure out.

Angie's Tyres and a Time Slip

It is almost twenty years since the following incident occurred, and it still feels unbelievable.

My medium friend, Angie Kruger, was staying with me for a long weekend break. During that visit, Spirit was definitely watching over us, particularly Angie.

The morning of Angie's last day was very ordinary. She was upstairs in the guest room packing, while I was preparing breakfast in the kitchen. It was raining heavily and was quite chilly outside. Angie and I had talked about running a psychic development workshop at my home later that year, and I was thinking about who we might invite, when suddenly a voice in my head said, "If you don't check her driver-side front tyre, she will have a fatal accident on the M4 between Port Talbot and Swansea and will never make it back here."

What an odd thing to say! I thought, presuming that the voice belonged to either Archangel Michael or Richie, Angie's Spirit guide. I decided to check the tyres when Angie came downstairs. Moments later as I listened to her footsteps walking along the corridor to the kitchen, a spontaneous image of a coffee stain on the sheet covering Angie's mattress popped into my head. Somehow, I had flipped forward in time and observed myself changing the sheets a few hours later.

"Don't worry, it's not gone through to the mattress," I said, as Angie walked into the kitchen.

Angie stopped short, a surprised look on her face. "How do you know I spilt coffee on the sheet?" she asked. When I told her I had flipped forward in time to when I was changing the sheets, Angie just said, "Oh, okay," as if it was something one did every day. Then again, we both knew that "down the rabbit hole" people are capable of some pretty weird stuff.

"Oh, and we have to check your tyres before you leave," I announced as Angie sat down to eat her egg on toast.

Angie grimaced. "It's raining. "I'm not going out there in that. And besides, my tyres are perfectly okay."

"Well, you're not having your egg until you've checked them," I said firmly. After a short argument, I marched Angie to her car, feeling like a parent dragging a rebellious child to the dentist. But her attitude soon changed when, on inspecting her tyres, we found a nasty split—exactly where my Spirit voice had warned me!

Angie was contrite and apologised for not listening, but she explained that her guide Richie had also told her she had a tyre problem and that she had taken the car to a garage before she left, and they had found nothing

How can one explain such a thing? One can't. But in conclusion, I believe our loved ones visit us after they have passed, particularly when there has been a loving connection in our lifetime, and we are in times of distress.

CHAPTER 9

Close Encounters of a Furred and Feathered Kind

Canine Cuddles

One morning, a young woman came to my clinic for a checkup after she had started a new relationship. As she sat down, the Spirit of a small black terrier jumped onto my lap and fell asleep in what felt like deep doggy contentment. I could sense his warm body and "saw" his curly black fur, but I instinctively let out a mini yelp of surprise when I first felt the pressure on my thighs. My patient asked if I was alright. I apologised, saying that a small black dog had just jumped on my lap and startled me. She glanced at my lap and said, "Don't worry, it's only Sooty. He was my late father's dog, and he is always jumping on people's laps." Nothing more was said; the dog disappeared and the rest of the consultation was normal. That was my first encounter with non-human, non-angelic spirits.

A second canine encounter occurred a few months later when I attended a post-graduate meeting at Neath Port Talbot Hospital. I joined my friend Margaret, one of the post-graduate secretaries, to eat lunch in her office before the meeting. Moments later, Margaret's friend Julie popped her head around the door to say hello after attending her mother's funeral. We invited Julie to join us for lunch, so she immediately headed next door to get a sandwich. After several minutes, I turned to Margaret and said, "I wonder why Jean is taking such a long time."

Margaret stared at me in shock. "Jean is Julie's mother's name," she said.

"Oh, maybe I misheard when you introduced her," I shrugged.

When Julie eventually returned, I was surprised to see a small white terrier-type Spirit dog following her. The dog rushed over to me, twining between my legs like a cat welcoming its owner home.

When I mentioned the dog's presence, Julie remarked that her mother had a white terrier who used to greet strangers by twirling around their legs.

I had never met Julie or her mother before. So, why had I called her by her mother's name? And how did I know her mother had a small white terrier? I can't explain what happened, but as with the black dog, the white dog disappeared as soon as I acknowledged his presence.

The Curious Case of Keston's Testicles

Keston was my second Jack Russell terrier. He came into my life due to a chance encounter with a woman called Miriam, whom I met while waiting to have a new tyre fitted in Swansea. It was a few weeks after my beloved Towser had gone to doggy heaven, and I was lost in my misery and started to weep. Miriam asked what was the matter. I sobbed as I told her about Towser, and she said that she had a friend in Oxford who had some tri-colour Jacks ready to be sold.

Towser had died the day before my birthday in May 1999, and we picked up Keston on my mother's birthday two months later. He was a doggy healer and made the grief from losing Towser at least bearable.

By the time Keston was seven years old, I was much more spiritually aware. One night, while I was deeply asleep, a Spirit helper, whom I believe was Archangel Michael, woke me up. The voice in my head said, "Keston has testicular cancer, and I want you to examine him immediately."

"I am too tired," I murmured sleepily. "I will check him in the morning."

But Michael was adamant. "Wake up and examine him now, you will forget to do it in the morning!" He said sternly.

Not wanting to get up, I reluctantly put my hand on the side of my bed where Keston was sleeping. As soon as he felt my touch, Keston rolled over onto his back, enabling me to gently palpate his testes as I had done to so many thousands of my patients over the years. Since I could not feel anything abnormal, I told Michael to stop worrying me. But he insisted I was wrong. "Examine him again," he ordered. I obeyed. But still, I could not feel anything amiss. Michael continued to nag me, so I repeated the process a third time. And on this attempt, I detected a small area in Keston's right testicle where I intuitively felt the energy of cancer. Suddenly, I was wide awake.

The next day, I took Keston to my vet and told him that I thought my dog had testicular cancer. I showed him where the lesion was, but he could not find anything abnormal. He was technically correct since, to my fingers, the cancer did not feel like an actual mass but more like an indescribable but nonetheless abnormal vibration.

How could I tell a left-brained vet that the previous night, an archangel had telepathically told me about the cancer? I wondered.

My vet was very professional. "Keep an eye on the area and bring him back if you are concerned," he advised. So I did, and when I returned a few months later, he apologetically agreed that there was a lump. Keston's tumour was removed the following day. A few years later, when Keston was suffering from an unrelated terminal illness and had to be put to sleep, he saw the same vet. Still apologetic, the vet recalled how I had picked up Keston's cancer several months before he did. On this occasion, I told him how I had known, and explained that he had no reason to apologise since I had angelic connections. To his credit, my vet understood. He is certainly my kind of vet.

It seems the Spirit realm even cares about our pets, and as you will see from the next encounter, I believe our late pets still care about us.

The Spirit Horse

I had my first, and so far only, encounter with the Spirit of a horse about 20 years ago. Amanda had been referred to me by a consultant gynaecologist for investigation of a possible infection. She had a history of inexplicable abdominal pain and had been fully investigated in the departments of gynaecology and gastroenterology. Nothing abnormal had been detected, and despite no significant risk factors for a sexually transmitted infection, I was asked to see her as a last resort.

Amanda was a petite woman with long, beautiful hair with distinctive, multi coloured tints. She gave me her medical history, which was unremarkable. Then, as we were talking, a horse Spirit sauntered into the room and started nuzzling the top of Amanda's head. I tried to ignore the horse and looked at Amanda to see if she was wearing any equine memorabilia, which I might have subconsciously taken in. I then checked her case notes for any horse-related details, but none were present. Meanwhile, the image of the horse was growing stronger and more overwhelming.

Its colouring was brown, white, and black, and his mane glinted with multi-coloured tints, similar to Amanda's hair.

I struggled to take an orthodox sexual history whilst looking at Amanda through the energy of a horse that was so intense I wouldn't have been surprised if it pooped on the clinic floor! I eventually overcame my fear of being thought insane and asked Amanda if she had ever owned a black, brown, and white horse with a multi-coloured mane just like her hair.

"Yes," she replied. "Only it was tan, black, and white, not brown."

"Did it like to nuzzle your head?" I asked.

"Yes. It always greeted me that way," Amanda said.

Seeing how unphased she was by my questions, I felt safe telling Amanda what I saw, adding that I believed her horse had come to give her love and strength. Amanda seemed comforted, the horse energy dissipated, and I was back in ordinary reality. Amanda explained that she had been married with children but was now divorced. I wondered if the stress of divorce might have caused her physical symptoms, but she said she was still good friends with her ex-husband, his new wife, and her children. I then examined Amanda and, like my colleagues, found no physical cause for her symptoms. I was puzzled.

"Is there anything else that could have upset you?" I asked.

Instantly, Amanda's demeanour shifted, and she opened up to confiding an unrelated traumatic family issue. "It really gutted me," she said.

The moment Amanda said the word "gutted," the penny dropped. Staring at each other in wonder, we both understood why she had been suffering from unexplained gut pain. We chatted about how stress and anxiety can cause a variety of abdominal symptoms, including irritable bowel syndrome (IBS). I advised her to seek counselling from her doctor and consider linking with healing equine energy by visiting the beautiful renowned Penclawdd salt marsh ponies who lived nearby.

Fortuitously, my patients were asked to complete a form about their clinic experience that day as part of our obligatory annual appraisal. Although the twenty or so forms were anonymous, Amanda signed hers saying that my telling her about the late pet horse had helped her understand the root cause of her pain and to realise what really matters in life.

A Jackdaw and a Long-Departed Jack Russell

Birds have long been associated with the occult and have been considered as messengers of the Gods and even as carriers of the Spirits of the departed. Many believe that feathers, especially white ones, are signs that a lost loved one is thinking about us and trying to bring comfort. White feathers are also considered to bring messages from angels during stress. A Google search shows how common these beliefs are even in people who spend their lives in ordinary reality. However, the belief that birds themselves can take over the consciousness of a dead person is far less prevalent. Birds most commonly associated with Spirit are robins, cardinals, and those in the Corvid family, particularly ravens, crows, magpies, and jackdaws. I have had a few experiences with this phenomenon, one of which is so bizarre I was initially reluctant to disclose it because I have no rational explanation for what happened.

My first bird experience, as described earlier, was of three ravens fluttering in my room when I was an inpatient at St. Thomas' Hospital in 1979. Since I was dosed up with painkillers, I put the experience down to a drug-induced hallucination. However, years later, I had another bizarre bird encounter involving the medium, Angie Kruger, whose Spirit guide, Richard, has a magpie totem animal. On this occasion, I was not on any medication, was tee-total, and was wide awake.

I met Angie decades ago when she gave a mediumship demonstration at Swansea Leisure Centre. Our first meeting was brief, but after that, our paths crossed at several Mind Body Spirit fairs. Since I was at the beginning of my reawakening, I was keen to learn as much as possible, so I invited her to my home in Swansea in June 2003. In my experience, one's ability to connect with Spirit varies daily, and mediums can have off days like anyone else (hence lots of room for sceptics to deride us). But when Angie visited my home, we were both in top form, and her presence enhanced my abilities.

Angie had driven a long way from her home in Cornwall, so the first evening was chilled. But at 6.15 a.m. I was awakened by someone or something scratching the pillow next to me. Angie was in the guest room on the floor above me. And being summer, my room was basked in sunlight, so I was not afraid. Thinking it was Angie's guide playing tricks, I said out loud, "Is that you, Richard? If so, give me a sign."

In less than a minute, I heard a crashing sound like someone throwing a bunch of keys at my kitchen window, just across the hallway from my bedroom. A few seconds later, I heard the crashing sound again. I rushed to the kitchen, and to my disbelief, a jackdaw was hurling itself at my closed kitchen window. The bird rammed the window twice more before I scared it off. Nothing like this had ever happened before—or since—and I had nothing shiny in the kitchen and no food to attract it.

That evening, after dinner, Angie and I discussed that day's and the previous night's events, and she went into a trance state so I could speak directly to Richard. We got on well, and I asked him why he had come into my bed and scratched my pillow. He told me it was my first Jack Russell, Towser, who wanted to visit. I remembered that Towser would always dig into my pillow when he wanted a cuddle, food, or a wee. How comforting! I then asked Richard if he had taken over the oddly behaving jackdaw's consciousness.

"Yes," came his response through Angie. "You asked for a sign, so I found the jackdaw and obliged you."

"Why not your totem bird, the magpie?" I asked.

"Where do you expect me to find a f---ing magpie at six o'clock in the morning?" He responded. I didn't know if Richie swore when he was alive. But I took some comfort in thinking our personalities might survive our transition to the next plane of existence.

Whilst my chat with Richard was memorable, I cannot comment on whether he was really present. But if he wasn't, my experience with the pillow and the jackdaw would be tough to explain.

Experiences like those I have described persuade me that the deep bond we forge with our pets does not die when they, or we, pass over. We've all been humbled by stories that tell of faithful pets who refused to leave a deceased owner's side or grave.

For example, the famous Greyfriars Bobby was a terrier whose story was made into several films. He apparently stayed by his owner's grave for fourteen years before he died aged 16 in 1872.

A Google search of the phrase "dogs who stay with their owners after death" reveals many modern heart-rending examples of canine loyalty. So why would such an ingrained trait not carry over into the afterlife? I hope so. I miss all my late pets.

Can Pets Communicate Telepathically?

Fido's Saviour

In 2010, my mum, who by then needed carers, was living with me and Fido, my third Jack Russell. Since I was still working as a full-time consultant, I arranged for carers to visit Mum daily. One day, when I was at work, one of the carers left my field gate open, and Fido escaped. Thankfully, help was on the way in the form of my friend Elizabeth Watkins. A keen dog lover, Elizabeth is a delightful, empathic woman with a large heart and a beautiful French accent. Elizabeth and I had trained in spiritual healing together. However, due to work and domestic commitments, we only saw each other occasionally

On the day Fido escaped, Elizabeth was visiting a garden centre just eleven kilometres from my house when she had a premonition that Fido was in trouble. Abandoning her shopping, Elizabeth raced to her car and drove to my house. She told me that every time she rationalized that her anxieties were probably unfounded, the car seemed to turn its wheel so that she continued towards my house and away from hers. Elizabeth arrived to see Fido, who was clearly lost, frantically running around at the far end of the village green. She called his name, and Fido raced towards her and jumped straight into her arms.

What was strange was that Elizabeth had started her journey to my house before my mum noticed Fido was missing. I have often wondered if this telepathic incident between Fido and Elizabeth was similar to that which Hans Berger and his sister experienced. Or was it just a bizarre coincidence?

According to world-renowned biologist Rupert Sheldrake, author of the book *Dogs Who Know When Their Owners Are Coming Home*, there is a strong telepathic connection between humans and animals that defies present-day scientific understanding. Sheldrake also believes that after-death communications (ADCs) with deceased pets is not uncommon and his research suggests that ADCs with non-human animals has parallels with human ADCs (see sheldrake.org). In my own limited experience, I think he's right. If this area interests you, I highly recommend Sheldrake's book, his website, and *Eternally Yours, Faithfully*, by Roy Radford and Evelyn Gregory.

I am also in agreement with the Psychic lawyer Mark Anthony, author of *The Afterlife Frequency*, who believes that animals have souls and are part of the collective consciousness. Mark Anthony's books and YouTube presentations are a must for anyone who wants to hear how science explains much of the occult, and his lectures are also exceptionally well presented and full of humour.

When Fido Met Brecon and Beverley

In November 2014, I snapped a ligament in my ankle whilst turning suddenly to put a log on my fire. I was on crutches for weeks, and the pain was so severe I was unable to drive. When I did start to mobilise, especially at night, it felt as if knives were cutting into the soles of my feet and salt was being rubbed into the wounds. I had developed a condition called *Plantar fasciitis* (PF). This severe pain continued for over a year, precluding sleep and any social life. I was depressed.

One morning, whilst hobbling around in my garden trying to give Fido a little fun playing with a ball, I felt I could not take any more pain and started silently weeping. I was alone and said out loud, "Oh Lord, I can't take this anymore, so please either take me or send someone to help."

My prayers were answered instantaneously when I saw a strange dog at my field gate. Fido immediately ran to greet it. I tried to follow him, but the pain in my feet felt like I was walking on hot coals, and my progress was very slow. I eventually reached the gate, where I found Fido wagging his tail at a beautiful female Scottish deerhound lurcher walking on the village green with his owner, Beverley. Apologising for being so slow, I explained to Beverley that I had PF, which was so bad that I had just prayed aloud for help. Bev looked startled, then confided that she had just returned to the UK from California, where she was a state-certified medical massage therapist specialising in treating PF.

We were both shocked by what seemed to be either an instant response to my prayer or one tsunami of a coincidence. We chatted for a while and arranged for Bev to return with her massage couch that afternoon. The massage lasted over three hours and left me sore in every muscle group. I felt bruised for three days, but the PF had gone and has never recurred. Had Fido been spiritually commissioned to help answer my prayer for assistance? Or was it just a fantastic coincidence? I had lost my PF and gained an excellent friend, and Fido and Bev's dog Brecon had many fun times together before Brecon sadly passed in Bev's arms in 2020.

Fido died unexpectedly in July 2022. He was my best friend, my canine guardian angel, and my *raison d'etre*. My comfort during years of coping with the stresses of work and supporting my demented mum, Fido had always licked my tears when life's challenges became overwhelming, and I was beyond consolation. For two nights before Fido became acutely ill, I'd had the same vivid nightmare. I dreamt that he was lying dead next to me in bed, and I gently lifted his body. I woke in a panic and grabbed the very much-alive Fido for a reassuring cuddle. I had never had such dreams and wondered if his soul had been warning me. When I later carried his still-warm body from the vet's, it felt exactly as it had in my nightmare. I felt constantly sick, could not tolerate food and developed severe stomach pain. I felt as though I had lost the will to live, and my doctor diagnosed gastritis, acid reflux and depression. But, unable to tolerate antidepressant medication, I felt my only hope was to self-medicate with a Jack Russell puppy.

Jasper! His name came to me the instant I saw him—I sometimes wonder if what I actually "heard" was the French phrase *J'espère*—"I hope," because Hope is what he gives me.

My grief over the loss of Fido led me to ask two friends, the medium Angie Kruger and Dr Penny Sartori, what they believe happens when a pet dies.

Angie Kruger

"Pets are family and the grief of bereavement is equally soul crushing, but there is a reason for that. We are all incarnated spirits on a journey - that goes for animals too. There is a lot said about "soul mates" and some people do get hung up on the popular romantic theories, but there is much more to a soul mate connection than that.

Some people we meet are part of our life/spiritual pathway. They are an intrinsic part of our journey. It's difficult to explain but I would say that soul families are like frog spawn. They are all individuals but are part of the same energy jelly. Symbiotic really. So, when a beloved pet passes over their loss can actually cause a wound at soul level. When soul mates connect, their energy becomes part of each other and when one is lost it's like a difficult birth with spiritual blood and tissue being torn apart.

A lot of orthodox religions say that animals have no souls and do not go into the afterlife, this is totally wrong. What would "heaven" be like with only people?

I have been a natural medium since I was a child, and have given readings since I was 14 (over 50 years). During that time I have had countless instances of deceased pets coming through to clients in readings.

I have had many instances of wild animals coming back to reassure or say thank you to a person who was there for them.

I have endless accounts of animals returning from the afterlife to reconnect with people who loved them or helped them in times of need. And dogs and cats, I find, stay loyal to their earthly loved ones after their passing."

Dr Penny Sartori
"Pets are sometimes present in NDEs but it's usually children who say they have seen pets. I think it's because children have little or no experience of losing an adult. One man who told me about his NDE said he was greeted enthusiastically by his late black Labrador."

Fido's death had a significant impact on my beliefs since, curiously, his death was harder to come to terms with than both my mother's and much-loved uncle's deaths in 2019. My mother and uncle were in their late 90's and frequently told me they wanted to pass over. Fido was a fit thirteen-and-a-half-year-old Jack Russell, and I expected to have him with me for at least another three to five years. I had to leave him at the vet's for overnight observation but was told that all being well, I could pick him up the following day. His little paws gripped my shoulders as I handed him to the vet. I asked if I could stay with him, but I was not allowed. I was not with Fido when he died, possibly in pain and alone that night. This still haunts me in the small hours of the night when thoughts return to preclude sleep.

Wordsworth put it beautifully in his poem *Surprised by Joy*, in which he expresses his emotions following the death of his little girl:

> *"That thought's return,*
> *Was the worst pang that sorrow ever bore*
> *Save one, one only, when I stood forlorn,*
> *Knowing my heart's best treasure was no more;*
> *That neither present time, nor years unborn*
> *Could to my sight that heavenly face restore."*

Unlike Wordsworth, who ended his poem by saying that he would never see his daughter's heavenly face again, I believe we will see our relatives, friends, and pets again. Though this is little comfort in the here and now. I feel ashamed that I grieve so much over a dog when there is so much suffering in the world, and I can only admire people's resilience and try to emulate it. Our pets are indeed sent to help us, and we can take consolation in knowing they are waiting for us.

CHAPTER 10

Psychometry Part One

The Psychometry of Objects and Places

If you Google "psychometry" you might find it defined as "the supposed ability to discover facts about an event or person by touching inanimate objects associated with them." I believe/know that not just objects but also places and people have energy fields that hold subtle information. Below are a few of my own experiences in accessing this consciousness and a discussion of a few other well-known examples of the phenomenon which defy rational explanation.

Regardless of whether we believe in ghosts, spirits, or poltergeists, many of us have had an experience where we have felt uncomfortable or uneasy in a particular place or around a person. I suspect that few of us would be keen to live in a house where a serial killer had lived or people had suffered tragic deaths. We may not be able to describe what is bothering us, but we all have a built-in sensor that tells us whether we feel comfortable or creeped out in certain places or around a particular person. We usually put it down to positive or negative energy.

When I was a teenager, I was one of two students from my school who were awarded an educational trip to Europe, which included a visit to the Plötzensee prison in Berlin, where Hitler hung some of the brave men who tried to assassinate him. The hooks on which the men had been hung like cattle were still there, and the building exuded an energy which felt like being embraced by agonising fear, pain and death. Many of us expressed the same feelings, and our group did not stay there long. I still shiver at the memory over half a century on.

When I contrast that with the feelings of awe and grace I experience when visiting cathedrals such as Wells Cathedral in Somerset or St David's in Pembrokeshire, where people have prayed and nurtured their souls for centuries, I can't help believing that people, objects, buildings, and places can retain imprints of information or strong emotions in their energy fields, which can be "picked up," sensed, or read by energetically sensitive people.

While there is no hard scientific evidence for the veracity of psychometry, I've witnessed many psychometric readings from psychics and mediums, and have sufficient personal experience to know that it is a real phenomenon. Here are just a few examples.

The Psychometry of Objects

A Tale of Two Watches

My much-loved Aunty Vi died in June, 2004. Soon after, my uncle gave me her watch, which happened to be identical to mine. As I held her watch, I sensed how different it felt from my own. My aunty Vi's watch radiated a soft and gentle energy whilst mine felt more assertive.

Curious about the difference, I conducted a little experiment. Placing the watches on a table for a few hours so they would both be settled to room temperature, I asked my uncle to close his eyes and then placed one of the watches in his hands. Without hesitation, he accurately identified his wife's watch. I then repeated the experiment with my mum, with the same result.

Since I loved my aunt dearly, I decided to wear her watch instead of mine. I found its presence extremely comforting in my grief. After several months, my aunt's energy dissipated, and I felt the watch had become my own. This is simple psychometry.

Strangely, back in 1985, long before I committed to studying consciousness, I'd had another "watch" experience. It was during one of my mother's visits to London, just before I left to take up my consultant post in Swansea. I had scheduled readings for us both with a medium in Wimbledon. Just before leaving my house, a letter arrived announcing that my sister in Devon had just had a baby. We were shocked at the news since we hadn't even known she was pregnant.

As my mother was a complete non-believer, I had arranged for her to be seen first so she couldn't accuse me of briefing the medium ahead of her. Mum emerged from her session looking both shocked and contrite. Apparently, the medium had asked if she could hold Mum's wristwatch to tune into her energy. On taking it, the medium said, "This isn't your watch." She was right. I had given the watch to my mother two weeks before. The medium then asked for my mother's glasses and within seconds told her that she had just had a grandson and even gave her my sister's married name.

∽

A Golden Ring and an Arum Lily

My first formal experience of psychometry took place in about 2002/3 when I attended an open circle at Townhill Community Centre with my medium friend, Gill. Townhill is in a relatively deprived area of

Swansea, which, reputedly, has a good community Spirit and splendid views of Swansea Bay. I found the people to be very nice, working-class, Welsh folk with mums not dissimilar from my maternal granny, whose character was forged by the poverty of the Welsh mining community she was raised in, the horrors of the First World War, and the desire to improve their children's lives through education.

Gill and I arrived at the community centre a bit late to find at least fifty people sitting in a circle with their eyes pinned on a large silk-scarf-covered plate being passed around. Some were taking items from the plate, but most were observing.

"Take an item," Gill whispered as the plate passed us. She didn't tell me that by doing what she said, I would be volunteering for a very public baptism into the art of psychometry—in other words, I had set myself up to give a reading. Luckily, there were three or four people ahead of me, so by the time they had performed their readings, I had got the gist of what was expected.

The object I had selected was a gold ring. Tossing it in my right hand and covering it with my left, I confessed that I had never done this before. "All I'm picking up is that whoever this belongs to has recently been to Stonehenge and had their photograph taken on a flat stone," I said. I then put the ring back on the plate, and the next person in the circle gave their reading of the item they had selected. It wasn't until later that Gill told me the ring I had been holding belonged to an acquaintance called Ann, who had verified everything I'd said.

A few weeks later, we attended another meeting at the community centre. On this occasion, we had been told to select and bring along a flower from our garden that we were drawn to. At the meeting, we all held our flowers as the group leader came around, chose one, and handed it to another person with instructions to tune into the vibes of the person who had picked the flower. She called this "flower psychometry." I was given an arum lily and told to share what I intuited about its owner. The moment it touched my hand, I was unexpectedly hit by an avalanche of sexual energy.

All eyes were on me, and all I could pick up was a whole lot of sex. Feeling pressured to say something, I found myself procrastinating as, for some inexplicable reason, and almost as if they had a mind of their own, my fingers were sensuously moving up and down the spadix (the penis-like spike in the middle of the flower).

"Go on," the group leader insisted.

"Well," I said hesitantly. "I am picking up that the person who picked this flower is enamoured with sex and very sexually active."

There was a sudden silence in the room, as dozens of faces gawped in shock at the awful, totally inappropriate statement I had just made. I was beginning to think that sex must definitely be a *"ych-i-fi"* (yucky) subject in this Welsh community when two vibrant ladies opposite, one of whose flower it was, came to my rescue. With peals of laughter, one of them admitted that, yes, she did indeed have a very healthy sex life.

"You mean, totally obsessed with it," her more forthright companion clarified with a knowing smirk.

The group leader was clearly not amused. I felt like a naughty schoolchild when he took me aside later and gave me a good telling-off. "You should have been mindful that there are children present." he chided.

"Well, you told me to share what I sensed," I reminded him, convinced nobody there had really been offended. But nonetheless, I was a little hurt. Feeling unwelcome, I chose not to return.

Crystal Balls and a Pair of Specs

Another experience of psychometry occurred in 2004 when I attended a five-day tarot reading workshop at the now-closed but awesomely beautiful Buckland Hall near Bwlch, not far from my home in Abergavenny.

As part of the workshop, each attendee was given a small numbered crystal ball, about two-thirds the size of a golf ball, with the instruction to carry it on our person all week and sleep with it under our pillow every night. I duly kept my crystal ball in my bra like an egg waiting to hatch. On the last morning of a fascinating week we were told to place our crystal balls into a box. The leader then took the box, chose balls at random, and handed one to each of us with a direction to write ten characteristics of the person who had kept that ball close to them throughout the week.

When it came to my turn, I was reluctant to speak. I told the group I did not want to publicly say what I had picked up since it was not very nice, but the leader didn't want to accept that. Finally, after much cajoling, with my words tripping over my tongue, I hastily recited everything I had written as if rushing my words would make the comments less unpleasant. Only to be told I was completely wrong by the lady whose ball I had read.

"I'm so sorry," I quickly apologised. Thankfully, the group were very supportive, and since we were all rookies, it didn't take too long to get over my embarrassment as we adjourned for lunch. Then, just as we finished our food, the lady whose ball I had read approached me and asked if we could step aside to talk. Fearing she may have been cross with me, I anticipated another telling-off. But, in fact, she had come to apologise for making me look foolish. "All ten things you said were true," she admitted. "I just didn't want people to know."

We chatted briefly, I gave her some counselling, and left, feeling very humbled by the experience.

My public presentations of psychometry invariably caused me some personal embarrassment, but one gets used to it. Folks at such meetings are pretty laid back, so when I attended a psychometry session at Bill Harrison's 2006 healing fair, I was pretty chilled.

I had a ticket for an hour-long Introduction to Psychometry Workshop and arrived early to get a good seat. The teacher gave us an introduction followed by several demonstrations of reading objects belonging to group members. When she asked for a volunteer and not one of the hundred or so participants raised their hand, I said I would be happy to step forward. The teacher scanned the group and then landed on a late attendee who had just arrived. "See if you can read her spectacles," she challenged.

As before, holding the spectacles, I was instantly infused with information about their owner. Since none of what I was receiving seemed positive, and mindful of my previous experiences when my subjects had denied what I had told them, I felt it wise to prepare the audience for my failure by claiming to be inexperienced. "Most of what I am getting is probably nonsense, anyway," I warned, before reluctantly reeling out a tale of woes.

As anticipated, the latecomer insisted that everything I'd said was wrong. The teacher said nothing, and feeling the mildly scornful eyes of the audience bouncing off my aura, I silently returned to my seat. I remained there until the class ended and I could escape to an "Everyone is Psychic Workshop" in a neighbouring tent.

An hour later, I emerged from the workshop. It was a blissfully sunny day, and I was strolling around, pondering what had happened, when I suddenly saw the leader of the psychometry workshop running towards me. "I've been looking around the field for you," she announced breathlessly. She said the lady with the specs had approached her after the event and asked if she knew me. "Apparently, everything you said in your demonstration was true and she now desperately wants to speak to you," the teacher said, pointing me towards a nearby tree where she had told the lady to sit until she found me. It was like a re-run of what had happened at Buckland Hall. Only this time, having qualified as a spiritual healer, I could also help the woman with orthodox counselling and energy healing.

King Richard III's Bones

Philippa Langley is a British writer, producer, and Ricardian who was awarded an MBE for her role in the now-famous "Looking for Richard project," which ended in the discovery and exhumation of Richard III in 2012. Philippa's story has now been turned into a book and a film titled "The Lost King." Philippa's discovery of the bones of King Richard III in a Leicestershire car park because of "an odd sensation" may also be a form of psychometry.

In May 2004, Langley visited several sites in Leicester, including the three car parks identified in 1975 as possible burial locations. It was at the northern end of one of the car parks that Philippa reported feeling "a strange sensation" coming over her and "knew in my innermost being that Richard's body lay there." In 2005, Philippa returned to the car park and experienced the same feeling. When she looked down, she saw that someone had painted a reserved "R" over the space, which, she said, "told me all I needed to know."

In an interview for "You" magazine, Philippa said, "It was a funny feeling. Like something coming up through my legs and my feet. It got stronger and stronger, so I felt almost faint. There, beneath my feet, was the letter 'R.' It was obviously for 'Reserved,' but I felt I was standing on Richard's grave."

I think that Philippa Langley may well have had a psychometric connection with King Richard's bones or maybe she had focused on him for so long that she had developed an energetic connection with his soul. Philippa's comment that the bones were found under the letter "R" is, logically, just a coincidence. Still, given her strange, inexplicable feeling over the grave, it's intriguing to muse that maybe Spirit was trying to make life easier!

I am sure that many sceptics would be inclined to dismiss Philippa's experience as an anomaly, a one-off, and, more likely, a mere coincidence. I wonder what they might make of this news: Philippa has now had a similar "odd sensation" whilst looking for the bones of King Henry I. In 2014, Philippa Langley embarked on a new project to locate the remains of Henry I of England, buried at Reading Abbey. That project, known as the "Hidden Abbey Project," fell apart. But in 2020, Philippa announced that she believed that the grave of Henry I was beneath the western car park of the now abandoned Reading Gaol, which famously once housed the poet and writer Oscar Wilde when he was serving a sentence for homosexuality. Ironically, that car park also contains a space marked with the letter "K." And on this occasion, Langley said that she felt "as if I was standing on someone's grave."

It will be interesting to see if Philippa Langley's suspicions are correct and if there really is a body buried beneath Reading Gaol's car park. I suspect Philippa is gifted with a sixth sense, and I look forward to possible future revelations.

The Psychometry of Places

Regarding the psychometry/consciousness of places, I confess that besides the contrasting emotions I felt when visiting Plötzensee prison and various places of worship, I have little personal experience of this phenomenon.

However, I am sure we have all sensed an unpleasant atmosphere when entering a room following an argument. While this could be a pheromonal response, it's not unimaginable that repeated actions such as prayers or executions in a building or location over decades might result in the walls/ground being imprinted with or absorbing the energy of those deaths or prayers. Lourdes is a very well-known example of the healing power of places, but less well-known is the idea that specific locations may harbour unknown forces which could affect the career choices of the local population. A prime example is the curious story of the Physicians of Myddfai.

What follows is garnered from various sources, including sections of the publication *Transactions of the Physicians of Myddfai* edited by Robin Barlow—especially chapters written by a former consultant colleague, Dr Don Williams, MD FRCPsych.

Myddfai is a small parish in the heart of rural Carmarthenshire in south west Wales. Its economy is based on agriculture and forestry, and it is a beautiful mountainous area with a mystical lake called *Llyn y Fan Fach*. It's the sort of place where, on a warm, misty day, one would not be surprised to see Merlin wandering along the shore of the lake, gathering herbs and casting spells. Indeed, the legend of the Myddfai physicians began at *Llyn y Fan Fach*.

There are many versions of this legend, but most agree that some time in the 13th century, a local shepherd boy herding his sheep beside the lake saw a beautiful young woman, a lake fairy, emerge from the lake. The shepherd fell in love with her, and she eventually agreed to marry him with the caveat that if he ever struck her three times without cause, she would return to the lake. Initially, all went well, and the couple brought up three sons. But eventually, the husband struck his wife three times needlessly, and she went back into the lake. Her sons would often return to the lake. One day, when her eldest son, Rhiwallon, was walking by the lakeside, his mother reappeared and handed him the medieval herbal equivalent of a medical textbook. She told him that he and his descendants would be healers. Thus began the physicians of the Myddfai dynasty, the bloodline of which evidently continued into the 18th century.

Since then, the number of doctors born in Myddfai has been disproportionate to the area's population. This phenomenon is eruditely confirmed by Dr Donald Williams, the eminent psychiatrist mentioned above, who grew up in the area, and is an Honorary Research Fellow at Swansea University. In a chapter Dr Williams contributed to the "Transactions of the Physicians of Myddfai Society," he enumerates a list of a modern-day cohort of physicians who were also born in Myddfai and concludes:

> "It is difficult to offer a satisfactory explanation for this phenomenon. Although no systematic data collection has been carried out it is not unreasonable to put forward the suggestion that this can be described as a clustering effect. It is very similar to the clustering of talents in the performing arts, which is evident in the Afon Valley and Port Talbot, the area that has produced Ifor Emmanuel, Richard Burton, Rebecca Evans, Anthony Hopkins, Rob Bryden, and now the remarkable Michael Sheen."

Dr Williams postulates that the tradition of the Physicians of Myddfai may have influenced the career choices of bright children in the area. However, I wonder if something more is at play. Could a specific kind of energy in the area attract souls destined to be healers? This may seem nonsense, but such hypotheses appear almost plausible when strolling around the dreamy lake.

Given my own improbable journey from an impoverished working-class child of post-war Britain, earmarked to inherit her mother's market stall and a life of hard physical labour to an academic doctor, I sometimes wonder whether I might have absorbed the desire to become a healer from my environment? According to David Tipper, author of the book *Stone and Steam in the Black Mountains*, the tin village built for the workers of the Grwyne Fawr reservoir included a hospital. My childhood tin shed home was part of that village, and I suspect the hospital may have been our home. But, of course, it's impossible to know if my tin shed, possibly ex-hospital home overlooked by the awesome Blorenge mountain, helped morph my fate into my destiny.

Whatever its aetiology, I know psychometry is real because of my own experiences outlined earlier. Although I have had only a handful, you only need to see a giraffe once to know—rather than believe—that it exists. In the next chapter, I will discuss medical intuition and the psychometry of people in health and disease.

CHAPTER 11

Psychometry Part Two

Medical Intuition—The Psychometry of People in Health and Disease

What is consciousness? Scientists, philosophers, and theologians have debated this question for millennia. And still, despite our enormous strides in understanding our universe, a definitive answer eludes us. So, I cannot give a scientific explanation for the experiences that I share in this chapter. What I can tell you is that my life experiences, research, and attendance at many consciousness workshops have led me to believe that our consciousness is not just an epiphenomenon of brain function but is an energy that is distributed throughout our bodies and that specific organs such as the heart, brain, and gut are probably the primary consciousness processors. After all, within orthodox medicine, the electromagnetic energy within and around us can be measured and assessed by electrocardiograms, electroencephalograms and electrogastrograms. I also believe this energy is not just confined to the physical body but extends into an aura around each person and probably much further into a space time continuum.

Cosmologist, futurist, and best-selling author of *The Cosmic Hologram – In-formation at the Centre of Creation*, Dr Jude Currivan, goes one step further with her explanation that "Consciousness is not what we have, it's what we *are*." If Dr Currivan is correct, that would explain how I could "tune into" and read, or pick up impressions from, the consciousness of the individuals mentioned in this and other chapters. I also believe that we all can "read" and glean information from the consciousness, or the auras, of those around us. I regard this ability as the psychometry of consciousness.

One question I am sometimes asked is if one can use psychometric methods to detect pathology in people? Psychometry typically involves using inanimate objects to determine either the history of the object or that of the people associated with it. Some people seemingly can "read" people's physical bodies, even at a distance or from a photograph. These people are often referred to as medical intuitives. One of the most acclaimed is Caroline Myss whose work I mentioned previously. In some respects, one could say this, too, is a form of psychometry.

When practicing psychometry, I would hold an object and observe any thoughts in my head. Over time, I also found that detecting an abnormality in a human or animal's body is possible using the same technique as inanimate psychometry. In fact, this concept is not as much at odds with orthodox medicine as one might imagine. Physicians use electroencephalograms and electrocardiograms to detect pathological changes in a patient's electromagnetic field, which in turn, relates to pathology in the underlying organ as in, for example, epilepsy or heart attacks. Psychometry also involves sensing subtle abnormalities in the aura around the human body. The difference is that the former relies on a person operating sophisticated technical equipment to obtain information, whilst the latter depends on the human mind and our so-far unseen and unlabelled abilities to "tap" into the same electromagnetic field. At the moment, conventional diagnostic methods are all we have since psychometry is not an exact science. Hopefully, when we have a greater understanding of the human energy field, scientists may eventually develop machines that can reliably detect a wider range of abnormalities. Professor Korotkov describes his research in this area in his book *The Energy of Consciousness* (see Recommended Reading). Meanwhile, the following are some of my experiences of intuitively reading people's minds and detecting pathology.

Reading a Stranger's Mind

In 2006, I attended a healing fair near Glastonbury, where I signed up for a workshop called Everyone is Psychic. We were told to hold both hands of a stranger sitting next to us, breathe into their heart for a minute, and then tell them what impressions we received. I was seated next to Janet, who had come with a friend, and both seemed to be having a jolly time. I told Janet that since this was the first time I had practised this exercise, my impressions may not make any sense to her. I then relayed my impressions, saying that I felt she had three children, but they weren't with her; she lived in a terraced house but also mucked out horse stables; was writing a book and had a challenging relationship with her husband. And I could smell a lot of baking around her. At each disclosure, Janet and her friend became more animated, and when I asked how much of what I had said was correct, they both chorused, "Everything!"

Janet had had three miscarriages, lived in a terraced house but had a horse in livery, she had been commissioned to write a children's book, was going through a tough time in her marriage, and used to be a professional baker.

A Sheepish Encounter with a Medical Student

It was the morning of July 24th, 2008. Nothing much paranormal had occurred for several weeks and I felt all too grounded in Newtonian reality as I briefly checked my emails before starting my morning clinic. I perked up when I was joined by Megan, a graduate entry medical student (GES) allotted a teaching session with me. I liked teaching GES's because they were highly motivated and usually had open but questioning minds, which were fun to interact with. Megan was no exception, and after briefly bonding over a quick cup of tea and a chat about our mutual interest in Welsh rugby, we started what was to be an intense four-hour female clinic. The clinic would alter Megan's view of reality and zap me briefly back into a quantum world where medicine is more about moving energy and less about drugs and surgery.

The clinic was busy, and I had to work allopathically and fast to keep the waiting times down, so there was no time for discussion between patients. All I knew of Megan's private life was that she came from a respected local family. The morning continued uneventfully with the usual mix of the "worried well," and patients with chlamydia, warts, yeast infection, etc. But then a very anxious patient came into my consulting room. I introduced Megan and asked if it was okay for her to stay. The patient was in her 30s and wanted a check-up but was too scared to be examined. I realised I could not spend too long with her with such a full waiting room. So I explained that I was a registered and insured spiritual healer and would she mind if I energetically calmed her down. I told her I would need her to hold my hands as we closed our eyes and symbolically breathed into each other's hearts. When she said yes, I asked her where she felt safe.

"In my back garden," she replied. I then took her in her mind to this safe place and anchored the feeling of calm for her imminent physical examination. When she said she felt much more relaxed, I quickly examined her. Curiously, Megan commented that she, too, had been affected and felt calmer.

The clinic continued uneventfully and ended at about 1.30 p.m. I adjourned to my office to find my lunch pack, and Megan followed to get her attendance record signed. As she was about to leave, she asked if I would show her what energy healing felt like. Sensing I was channelling well that day, I placed my hands vertically on either side of her outstretched right hand. Megan's reaction was almost instantaneous. "I can feel a soft electric current coming from your palms," she said, her eyes wide-open with shock. As I closed my eyes and tried to channel healing energy into Megan's hand, I was instantly transported to a time when she was delivering lambs. I had a sense of kneeling on wet grass, the soft, warm membranes of a newly-born lamb running between my fingers like frogspawn. Looking deeply into Megan's eyes, I asked, "Have you ever delivered lambs? And have you considered becoming a midwife?"

The look on Megan's face was priceless. "How did you know that?" she asked in stunned amazement.

I explained that I believed consciousness was loosely linked with one's physical body and that her hands held part of a very positive, conscious experience she'd had, which had blended with my energy field and been decoded in my brain. I then scanned Megan's hand on its dorsal surface (with my right hand palm down) and felt a slight electromagnetic disturbance (a prickly sensation, like a day-old nettle sting) over the joints. When I asked Megan if she had any arthritis in the joints, she said no, but that her gran had told her she may get arthritis because

Megan's fingers were the same distinctive shape as her gran's, who had developed the condition.

Megan then related an experience she'd had as a teenager when staying with a school friend whose dad was a shepherd. One day, when the shepherd was away, a sheep had dropped its lamb in front of Megan and her friend. Since the shepherd's daughter was squeamish, Megan had stepped in to save the lamb struggling to free itself from the membranes.

"It was a wonderful experience," Megan confirmed. "And, yes, I did consider becoming a midwife, but then decided to read medicine instead."

I have had similar experiences of consciously and spontaneously entering someone's consciousness many times. I believe that empathy with one's patients is a kind of consciousness sharing, part of the ritual of creating a sacred healing space. So much attention is now paid to a reductionist tick-box approach to patient management that the power of the physician's presence is often overlooked and undervalued. The energy in the sacred space can sometimes help with reaching a diagnosis and healing… what I would call honouring the Shaman within.

The Man who Transferred his Grief to His Gonads

One such incident occurred in 2006 when a new specialist registrar named Laura, whose previous background was in gynaecology, had just joined us. One morning, soon after Laura's arrival, she saw a young man who had been suffering from unexplained testicular pain for several months. Laura asked for my intervention since she was unsure how to help him. The man's pain had been extensively investigated from an infectious disease angle and in the department of urology and orthopaedics. No cause had been found, and he had little in the way of risk factors for undetected STIs.

I examined his testes and, like my colleagues before me, could find no physical abnormality or clinical cause for his pain. It was all rather odd, I thought, as I sifted my memory for similar cases. Without thinking about it, I had kept my right hand above the patient's testes. Suddenly, a bolt of energy pulled me out of my trance. I felt as if I had been energetically whacked in my heart with a bolt of despair and wanted to cry. I looked into the patient's eyes and said, "There is something wrong here; the pain is not in your testes; it's in your heart. You have a symbolic hole in your heart. Why is your heart sad?"

The poor chap instantly burst into tears as he spluttered that the pain had come on at the exact moment the love of his life had left him. Since few medical conditions, apart from trauma or torsion of the testicle, cause this type of acute onset pain, I explained that Western medicine had investigated him as far as possible, but I could arrange psychosexual therapy. When he asked how I knew about the emotions he was suffering, I told him about my training as a spiritual healer. He immediately calmed down, saying he felt much better now that he understood. Although we offered him further appointments if the pain persisted, he said he no longer needed this, and that was the last I saw of him.

When Laura looked bemused, I explained that he was so upset with the loss of his partner that his heart could not stand the pain, so he transferred it to his testes like a ball of dark energy. Of course, I told her, we must always follow the Western route regarding diagnosis and therapy until the final brick wall has been reached. Only then can we look for more subtle causes of symptoms. To do otherwise would risk missed diagnoses and possibly even litigation.

Banishing Lucy's Tummy Pain: Magic? Miracle? Or Placebo?

In 2007, a patient came to see me accompanied by a friend she had invited along for support. The friend, Lucy, sat quietly by as I conducted my examination. While I was talking to my patient, I suddenly felt a stabbing pain in my stomach that I instinctively knew was not my own. The energy seemed to be coming from Lucy. So, out of curiosity, I asked Lucy if she was experiencing any abdominal pain. She wasn't holding her tummy or grimacing, so it was a bit of a long shot. But she said that she was indeed suffering from long-standing stomach pain that had been thoroughly investigated by the gastroenterology department. Unable to find any concrete cause, Lucy had been told that it was very likely anxiety and that nothing could be done. Interestingly, the moment she acknowledged the pain was hers, my pain disappeared!

Since it was close to lunchtime, and I had no other patients until after my break, I asked Lucy if she would like some energy healing. Figuring that since I had energetically picked up her pain, it was something I was destined to help alleviate, I held my left hand on her head and my right hand near, but not touching her stomach. I sensed the pain was emanating from the subtle energy field around Lucy's abdomen and had not yet manifested as a detectable physical illness, hence the negative orthodox screening tests. The laying on of hands lasted just a few minutes, and I never saw Lucy again. However, several months later, I received a letter from her outlining all the symptoms and tests she'd had before meeting me, and her subsequent surprise at my offer of energy healing.

Lucy candidly wrote that she hadn't expected anything from it, but, being open-minded, was content to give it a go. A week passed without any change, and then she woke up one morning, astonished to feel no sickness and no horrible feeling in her stomach. Another week passed, then a month without recurrence of her former symptoms. "I told anyone who would listen about my experience," she wrote. "I have a busy lifestyle, and I'm tired now and again, but nothing compared to what I had experienced for a year and a half. So thank you, from the bottom of my heart."

I do not know if Lucy's recovery was natural, related to my intervention, or simply a result of the placebo effect, possibly enhanced by her positive affirmations in telling so many people what had happened.

The Trainee GP, her Late Mother, and the Hedge Witch

Another odd encounter occurred when a trainee GP attended my clinic to learn the basics of GU Medicine as part of a Family Planning course and her late mother came with her.

"Good morning, Dr Blackwell," she announced. "My name is Kate. I am a GP on the Family Planning Course, and I am booked to sit in your clinic this morning."

I had come into work early to do some admin before I had to start teaching and felt slightly irritated that the interruption meant I could not deal with any emails before starting clinical work. Fortunately, all traces of irritation dispelled the moment I looked up to see the young woman in front of me, who seemed to be genuinely nice and enthusiastic about being in my clinic.

"Good," I said. "It's Anona, and may I call you Patricia?' The moment I said it, I floundered. *What? Why had I called her Patricia when she had just told me her name was Kate?* I wondered as my rational brain scurried for a "get out of jail card" to cover my mistake.

Without a moment's hesitation or the slightest change in her demeanour, Kate answered, "That's fine. Patricia is my late mother, who is always with me." We both chuckled as I explained that such occurrences were not uncommon in my practice. When Kate assured me that she was not alarmed and had, in fact, trained in Reiki healing herself, I knew we were in for a bit of a roller coaster ride with Spirit that morning.

Once in the clinic, Kate and I soon bonded as we discussed patients' clinical signs, differential diagnoses, and management plans. The first few patient encounters were unremarkable and entirely within orthodox practice. Then, everything changed when a patient in her late 30s entered the consulting room.

People with Spirits close to them often have a subtle glow around them, and I sensed this quite strongly with this lady. A gentle, motherly soul with an air of anxiety about her, Angela had been diagnosed by a gynaecologist with a benign but painful problem which affected one side of her pelvis. She had no risk factors for infection but had decided to be checked since, if pelvic infection was the cause of her pain, there might be some hope of relief.

There are many causes of abdominal/pelvic pain, from infection of the bladder, fallopian tubes or appendix to twisted cysts, ectopic pregnancy, endometriosis, Crohn's disease, ulcerative colitis or irritable bowel syndrome. Over the years, like most doctors, I had developed an intuitive sense of what was wrong with a patient by the subtle energies each condition created. It's not rocket science, but to put it simply, if you have an infection, you are likely to look and feel ill just as you would when you have a cold or flu. But if you have a non-infectious though potentially fatal condition, such as an ectopic pregnancy, you will look and feel more anxious than ill. Likewise, patients with, say, irritable bowel syndrome tend to look more irritable than either anxious or ill.

Over the years, I learned to respect the vibes I sensed and employ them in conjunction with orthodox history-taking and examination to assess what was happening. This respect for and faith in my intuition came partly from a serious incident early on in my career when I was a junior registrar at St. Thomas' Hospital in London in the mid-1970s. It had such a massive impact on me, the memory had never faded.

I had come on duty at noon one day and was taking over from a doctor who had done the morning session. Anxious to go off to his lunch, he asked me to finalise a patient he had seen by dispensing antibiotics for pelvic inflammatory disease (PID), which he had just diagnosed. After insisting that it was "just a barn door case of PID" and I only had to give her the diagnosis and antibiotics, I very reluctantly agreed.

The patient, a vivacious young girl in her twenties, appeared to me to look rather more anxious than ill. So, to exclude a potentially fatal ectopic pregnancy, I decided to go over her sexual history. She assured me that her periods had been normal, regular, and not late. But still, something nagged at me, and my intuition told me to beware. When I quizzed her about contraception, she reported that she'd had the same partner for several years and felt she could not conceive. Since today's rapid pregnancy tests that give instant results were not yet available and pelvic ultrasound was still in its infancy, there was no quick fix for my concerns. Torn between taking the easy and logical option of accepting my colleague's diagnosis and dispensing the antibiotics and the intuitive nagging of my deeply uncertain gut, I decided to contact the on-call senior registrar in Obstetrics and Gynaecology.

This was an era when senior registrars were granted almost the same demi-god status as consultants, and as a very junior registrar, I was at the bottom rung of the hierarchy. As if that weren't bad enough, I was doubly hindered by the fact that GU medicine was considered a low-status speciality. Thus, to ask a demi-god in a much higher-status speciality to admit a patient for observation and a pregnancy test when orthodox algorithms would preclude this being appropriate, was a very risky thing to do as, given the patient's history, I would appear incompetent and lacking in clinical acumen.

Unsurprisingly, the telephone discussion with the senior registrar went exactly as I predicted, and his frustration at being called away from his work by such trivia was clearly evident. "Just give the patient antibiotics and send her home," he insisted.

"But I'm worried she might collapse on the street," I pressed nervously.

"But she has not missed a period," he countered, his frustration and irritation becoming more palpable by the minute.

"Yes, but she looks anxious and not ill," I said, realising even as I said it that admitting that my diagnosis was based on perceived emotions certainly did not help my argument. I was losing the battle. In desperation, I played one last risky card. Agreeing to his suggestion politely, I said, "Okay. But I need to record your name in the notes, just in case I'm right and the patient dies."

The line went quiet. Suddenly, the air between us was thick, and there was a very pregnant silence as I sensed the senior registrar reassessing the situation. We both knew that I had effectively put his balls on the chopping block and, although the chopper would never fall if he was right, that was no longer a risk he could take.

After several long sighs, he reluctantly agreed to admit her. My gamble had paid off. But even as I made the arrangements to send the patient up to the ward, I couldn't help feeling a tremor of fear at the thought of future interactions with a demi-god whose feathers I had thoroughly ruffled and plucked.

Later, I phoned the ward to ask about my former patient.

"She's okay," a nurse told me. "But it was a close call." My patient had been put into a side room to await examination by the senior registrar. At a routine check, she was found to be unconscious with a blood pressure of 50/0. An ectopic pregnancy was confirmed and, presumably helped on its way by the pelvic examination my colleague had carried out that morning, had burst with near-catastrophic consequences.

After that episode, I never had trouble getting patients admitted and though I never faced a similar clinical situation again, my golden rule became that whenever orthodox and gut-made diagnoses conflicted, one must always delve deeper. Which is precisely what I knew I must do with Angela.

After taking Angela's history, I carried out routine tests for sexually transmitted infections. Then I explained that I would need to perform a bimanual pelvic examination to assess her pelvic organs. I conducted the examination whilst simultaneously narrating for the benefit of both my trainee and Angela what I was doing and what I could feel.

Angela had findings consistent with a benign, non-infectious condition, but sensing there may be a spiritual/emotional component to her condition, I wanted to be sure that what I sensed in her energy field matched the orthodox clinical diagnosis. Without thinking about it,

I spread my right palm out and automatically started scanning her lower abdomen, moving it in a circular motion about an inch above her skin, first over the painful side of her abdomen and then over the other side. I didn't recall having done this before, but I knew that I was in a slight trance state, and since part of me was aware that Angela and Kate might think I was crazy, I started to explain what I was doing.

Almost instantly, Angela interrupted me. "No," she said. "There is no need to explain. I know exactly what you are doing. I am a hedge witch."

The vibrations from the affected side of Angela's pelvis were distinctly different from the normal side. Wondering if Kate could sense the difference, I invited her to copy what I had done. To Kate's surprise and mine, she was aware of a difference between the two sides, only instead of describing what she felt as "happy" and "sad," as I had done, she used the terms "light" and "dark."

Angela confirmed that we were both right and that her physical condition had an emotional component: she felt upset about a previous miscarriage, and although her physical condition was causing the pain, her emotions were making it more difficult to cope. She spontaneously hugged us both as she left. We had not done anything medically to help but had allowed her to express her inner fears and hopefully made her life a little easier.

Can Consciousness Remain Within Our Organs?

Another fascinating type of possible psychometric phenomenon is cellular or transplant memory; this is a rare but intriguing phenomenon in which transplant recipients occasionally acquire memories and behaviour patterns that belonged to their donor. A paper by Sandeep Joshi entitled "Memory Transference in Organ Transplant Recipients"[*] reviews and discusses the work of the late neuropsychologist and author Dr Paul Pearsall, who collected organ transplant recipients' accounts. Pearsall, who was known for counselling individuals who underwent heart transplantation, claimed that these patients experienced significant and inexplicable changes in personality in which they became more like their donors in temperament and personal preferences, including changes in the food and music they liked, and even their gender preferences.

Joshi notes that:

> "Dr Pearsall has observed that heart transplant recipients seemed to be more susceptible to personality changes. Patients who had undergone organ transplants for kidney or liver also sensed changes in their sense of smell, food preference, and emotional factors but these changes were usually transitory and could be associated with medications and other factors of transplantation."

Joshi concludes his paper by discussing possible sceptical and alternative explanations for cases of transplant memory, which, among several

---

[*] Published in the Journal of New Approaches to Medicine and Health, volume 19, issue 1, 24th April, 2011

other theories, include psychometry theory in which he notes that some psychics suggest that the heart of the donor is imbued with the psychic energy of the donor, much like a ring or other object.

Joshi further notes that the biologist Lyall Watson suggested that:

> "Physical items with which we are in intimate contact can indeed take on our emotional fingerprints and store our thoughts and feelings. If plants and inanimate objects can store our feelings and thoughts, it is possible that our body organs, which are most intimately connected to us, also contain our emotional imprints."

For readers who, like me, find the possibility of cellular memory mind-blowing, I thoroughly recommend *The Living Energy Universe* by Gary Schwartz and Linda Russek. In it, they describe more of Dr Pearsall's research, including the case of an eight-year-old girl who received the heart of a murdered ten-year old-girl. The recipient subsequently had nightmares about how the donor had died and was able to give the police precise details of the murder so that the killer was caught and convicted. The authors add, "The time, weapon, place, clothes he wore, what the little girl had said to him… everything the little heart transplant recipient had reported was completely accurate."

I lack personal experience of transplant memory. But, serendipitously, as I was writing this, I spoke to a medical acquaintance who shared that a patient who'd had a bone marrow transplant from her sister developed her sister's aversion to fish and bananas.

I don't have any firm beliefs as to how transplant memory may be explained within orthodox medical thinking, but Joshi mentions the work of the pharmacologist Candice Pert, who proposed that "neuropeptides which are stored in every cell act as a sort of biochemical correlate of emotion… which could explain some forms of cellular memory." However, if transplant memory is a real phenomenon, our current medical model of consciousness is clearly inadequate.

The Psychometry of Hugs and the Human Aura

I am, by nature, an archetypal empath and a hugger. I have three power animals within shamanic traditions—bear, the healer; wolf, the teacher; and coyote, the trickster-teacher. As an empath, I am naturally drawn to comfort those who are suffering. I have learned that physical contact isn't always necessary. I believe that human energy fields can blend, auras can overlap, and the subtle vibrations of healing can be transmitted to anyone through the power of intention and focused thought. For many years, this happened automatically unless I was unwell or feeling particularly anxious. But somehow, my clairvoyance and my sensitivity to others disappeared when my dear demented mum came to live with me, and it's only very slowly returning. I believe this ability enabled me to tune into the young man I met at a dinner party who had urethritis and to detect the Spirit of the boy who walked through my clinic wall. Similarly, the energy of the trauma of sexual abuse can be so strong that I could pick it up just by sitting next to someone who had suffered such an awful experience.

Sometimes, one can sense the sorrow in a person's soul just by hugging them. To me, it feels like they are wearing a dark raincoat soaked in tears. It is particularly heart-breaking when I energetically encounter someone who has lost children and those who have suffered childhood abuse. I have the utmost respect and compassion for such people. Losing a dog is extremely painful, so to lose a child must bring sorrow beyond belief.

In conclusion, I believe consciousness is not just associated with the physical brain but is loosely associated in and around our bodies with epicentres of activity in the brain, heart, and gut, where it can be read by medical intuitives and, eventually, possibly technology. We will discuss this in a little more detail in the next chapter.

CHAPTER 12

What I *Know* Vs. What I *Believe* About the Paranormal

Part One: What I *Know* is Real

- Is consciousness confined to our brain? Or does it extend beyond our physical body?
- Does consciousness survive death?
- Is it genuine mediumship or a psychic message?
- Future memories—can our consciousness flip to the future?
- Can our pets communicate after death?

From birth, we are indoctrinated by our family and friends, and as we grow, we inevitably become brainwashed from exposure to many sources from books, school and church to television, radio, films, and social media.

As a child, I believed in Santa Claus and the tooth fairy because my mother told me they existed, and later, I believed—at first, unquestioningly—what my teachers taught me. Over the years, some of those acquired beliefs were discarded. But others became the filters through which I perceived and reacted to the world. These were primarily beliefs about religion and acceptable social behaviour. Still, they were just beliefs and not necessarily based on personal experience.

It is easy to confuse beliefs with actual knowledge. For example, I *believe* Australia exists because I have seen it on television, read about it in books, and have friends who have been there. Thus, the overwhelming evidence is that Australia exists, so I accept it does. But I don't actually *know* that it exists in the way that I know the chair I sit on exists because I've never been to Australia. The same applies to my paranormal experiences—there are some things I *know* and some things I *believe* based on limited personal experience and/or the balance of evidence from other sources.

Let's start with what I *know*:

Is Consciousness Confined to our Brain? or Does it Extend Beyond our Physical Body?

I know consciousness is not confined to our brain because I've had numerous experiences of tuning into other people's consciousness simply by being near them. For example, when I tuned into the thoughts of the young man at the dinner party who was anxious about having a sexually transmitted disease. And when I somehow "read" the teenage memories of the medical student concerning her life-changing delivery of a lamb in her youth. And when I diagnosed the cause of a patient's testicular pain as transferred heartache.

The concept that we live within/produce a dynamic electrical field around us is not new, and even within conventional medicine, measurement of the body's electrical field has become a routine diagnostic tool in several specialities. These include electrocardiography, developed by Willem Einthoven in 1901, which measures changes in electrical activity in the heart (electrocardiograms, ECGs) and electroencephalography (EEGs), which, as mentioned earlier, was invented by Hans Berger in 1929 and is used to detect abnormal electrical activity in the brain.

Furthermore, in a paper entitled "Biofield Science and Healing: History, Terminology, and Concepts," Rubrik and colleagues discussed how biofield research has shown that the electromagnetic field generated by one person's heart can affect another person's EEG.*

The authors noted that:

"While the ECG and EEG are readily detected from the body surface, the heart's magnetic field, generated by moving electric charges associated with electrical activity, can be recorded up to several feet from the body surface via a magnetocardiogram. Magnetic fields produced by the heart appear to carry information that may be detectable by other persons or animals. An example of the informational potential (bio effectiveness) of these heart fields is cardiac-induced entrainment (or frequency locking) detected when the R-waves of one subject's ECG become precisely synchronized with the onset of EEG alpha waves of another subject at a distance up to 5 feet."

This is cool technical stuff, but my take on the above is that it shows that orthodox research has found that one person's heart-generated electromagnetic field (which is, in turn, affected by the individual's emotional and physical state) can affect another person's consciousness as indicated by changes in the recipient's EEG. Hence, our consciousness is verifiably not just confined to our physical body but is energetically present in an electromagnetic field around us.

The discovery of Electrogastrography, which detects myoelectrical signals generated by smooth muscle in the gastrointestinal tract, is

---

* Glob Adv Health Med. 2015 Nov; 4 (Suppl): 8–14

attributed to Walter C. Alvarez, who produced the first human electrogastrograms (EGGs) in 1921. Thus, within the last century, even orthodox medicine has become aware of the body's energy field and how the measurement of its characteristics can aid in non-invasive diagnosis. It is also well-recognised that changes in our consciousness, e.g., stress, anxiety, etc., can directly impact our physiology and cause measurable changes in the electrical activity in the heart, gut, and brain.*

I believe modern medicine has become too mechanistic. Until we look at disease from physical, energetic, and spiritual aspects, we will continue to pursue costly and often toxic treatments for vibrationally established diseases rather than seek ways of detecting disease in our energy field before it manifests clinically. We need to adopt a new medical paradigm that recognises that many disease processes begin as energy forms, which only become evident when their vibration reaches the level of matter—as illustrated by my experience with my Jack Russell's testicular cancer. Until this happens, medicine will continue to drown in the clutter of expensive and sometimes outdated disease management rather than proactively pursuing disease prevention. Except for congenital disorders and traumatic injury, medicine should aim at maintaining wellness, not just mainly treating illness. This is not a new concept, but we will remain trapped in the materialistic healthcare model until we have reliable methods for detecting, analysing, and repairing the human energy field/aura.

---

* Go to www.heartmath.com for a more detailed understanding of the heart brain connection. *The Heartmath Solution* by Doc Childre and Howard Martin with Donna Beech is also worth reading.

In 1989, the late scientist and Professor Emeritus of the Department of Physiological Sciences at UCLA, Dr Valerie Hunt, published her book *Infinite Mind,* in which she wrote:

"Probably all diseases are connected with a disturbance or break in the flow in the energy field; this is functionally transferred to the organ system with ultimately destructive consequences. By the time organ systems are involved, degenerative changes are already occurring. In the future, we should be able to diagnose field disturbances by an aurascope and treat them months or years before they upset physical tissue."

Sadly, Dr Hunt's prediction has not yet manifested. When/if it does, massive healthcare savings in reduced drug use and hospital admissions would inevitably follow.

Does Consciousness Survive Death?

There are two reasons why the question of consciousness surviving death appears in this *I know* section. The first is that there is a plethora of scientific and empirical material on the subject. For example, an Amazon search for books on After Death Communication flagged over 600 volumes featuring personal experiences of this phenomenon, whilst a search for scientifically conducted studies on this subject realised numerous credible studies.

The second is because I have personal experience of this phenomenon, having either sensed or seen several people's deceased relatives or pets.

Fortunately, on each occasion there was a strong loving relationship between the person and the Spirit during life. I find it interesting that when I saw the human and animal Spirits, they appeared in colour and were mostly as you would see them in this reality.

It's hard to describe, but the emotions of the Spirits have also affected me. For example, when my consciousness was overshadowed by the mother of the lady who was drug raped, I felt an overwhelming feeling of frustration because she could not directly comfort her much-loved daughter. Love is a high-vibration emotion which, in my case, seemed to be a prerequisite for me to communicate with deceased people and pets.

Aside from my mediumistic experiences, I have attended countless spiritualist meetings over the decades where visiting mediums gave short messages to congregation members. I have also had dozens of private sittings. Sometimes—indeed, several times—I have even given the medium a reading when they've had a bad day.

On one such occasion a few years ago, I saw a medium at a local Mind, Body, Spirit Fair that could not link with Spirit. When she apologized, I said, "Don't worry." Then I surprised her by saying, "But Spirit has just told me you have a low calcium level and need to see a doctor."

"You're right," she confirmed. "My doctor has just done some tests, and I do have a low calcium level."

Of the many readings I have had, a number were poor, several were quite good, and a handful were breathtakingly accurate. One of the latter was with Jane Hutchinson. Jane's group, The Forget Me Not spiritual group, holds meetings on alternate Sunday mornings in Hereford and has a congregation of lovely souls, reflecting Jane's humble and loving personality. I don't often get a message, but the uplifting energy of the group is more than enough to justify dragging myself out of bed on a Sunday morning for the 45-minute drive to Hereford.

I have also observed many talented mediums at Jane's meetings and seen first-hand how accurate some messages are. One medium I recently watched addressed a man who had never met her. Yet she told him his late father's name, that he'd had a Jack Russell who used to hang on to his trousers, and even the unusual name of his dog, all of which he later told me was correct.

At another recent meeting with a visiting medium who lived some distance away, I watched for over an hour as she gave members of the congregation precise names of relatives and convincing details of unusual hobbies that she couldn't possibly have known. Her communications were so accurate that many cried tears of profound appreciation. I have noted that the clarity of the medium's link to Spirit seems to be directly related to the number of paper tissues needed. It was a joy to see so much grief lifted.

A word of warning though: if you decide to see a medium, be very selective, especially if you are new to this type of experience. Some may not have actual contact with Spirit but just be skilled at giving cold readings where they make general statements, ask leading questions, or give high-probability guesses and observe your response. I feel uneasy when a medium says something like, "I have a gentleman here in uniform. Can anyone take it?" Depending on the demographics of the audience, varying numbers of people will raise their hands and the medium may then say something like, "He's smoking and has a dog with him." Usually at least one person will have such a relative and the medium can then ask more questions and read the person's body language. When a medium says something that is wrong they often suggest that the event may happen in the future.

Rarely, a medium may even give alarming predictions causing a great deal of distress. Several decades ago, I saw an elderly medium who told me my mother would die in September of that year. It was already June, and I was distraught since the medium had been accurate about several other aspects of my life. When I asked her if she was sure, she said she was "almost always right." Mum lived for 20 years beyond that prediction, but I had several months of torment until September had passed. So I would recommend asking for advice about any medium you are considering seeing and maybe even attending a spiritualist church to see them in action first. I resonate best with mediums that give correct names and go to specific people in the congregation rather than just describing a nameless Spirit and asking if anyone can take them. I have also noted that the mediums who charge the most are not always the most accurate. Humble souls like Jane, who give their time because they want to use their gift to help people are often the most connected and compassionate.

Is it Genuine Mediumship or a Psychic Message?

It's sometimes difficult to distinguish between psychic messages and genuine mediumship. Whenever I received information psychically, I knew I was tuning in to a person's consciousness—their energy field, if you will. As with the young man whose sexually transmitted infection was dominating his mind at the dinner party, it was not usually an intentional intrusion on my part. But when it occurred spontaneously with patients, I think it was because the sole intention of our interaction was to help them. Whether they were aware of it or not, we were clearly energetically connecting because I could sometimes feel their pain in my body.

Mediumship is different in that one is tuning into the consciousness of a dead person. It's hard to describe this kind of connection, but I could feel subtle differences that "told" me the gender of the person I was connecting with. I could also place the Spirit's presence spatially. Most often, I would sense their energy slightly behind and to the right of me.

On rare occasions when I have sensed angelic energy, it was always of a much higher frequency—which is palpable but impossible to describe. Unlike the Spirits of "people," which I sensed were usually at ground level and to my right, angelic visitations always seemed to be slightly behind and above me.

Finally, whilst I can't explain how mediumship occurs or how I once was able to receive messages from "dead" people and occasionally pets, I can definitely add this to my "know" category.

Now, before you start wondering whether I've really lost the plot here, take note of this:

"The Phenomenology and Impact of Spontaneous and Direct After-Death Communications (ADCs)" is the name of an on-going, multi-lingual research project that started in February, 2018.[*] This study is conducted by a stellar team of investigators and led by Evelyn Elsaesser, an internationally recognised expert on death-related experiences. The first study involved English, French and Spanish experients whilst a later survey was in German and another is currently being conducted in Chinese.

Elsaesser's team developed an extremely detailed questionnaire about all aspects of ADCs, which was available online for six months in the

---

[*] https://www.evelyn-elsaesser.com/wp-content/uploads/2020/02/Booklet_Web_English_Research.pdf

respective languages. The findings of the surveys to date are available on the project website at www.adcrp.org. But here are some fascinating highlights.

The first survey in English, French and Spanish yielded over 1000 completed questionnaires and showed that ADCs take various forms with:

- 34% of respondents *sensing* the presence of the deceased
- 43% *hearing* the deceased either by external sound or by telepathy
- 48% *feeling* a physical contact
- 46% *seeing* the deceased, and
- 28% *smelling* a fragrance characteristic of the deceased
- In addition, 62% had an ADC during sleep/falling asleep or just waking up. According to those experients, "contacts that occur during sleep are completely different from an ordinary dream."
- And, lastly, 21% had a "crisis ADC"—i.e., when, for example, the deceased came to say goodbye, as happened to me when I was a junior doctor at St. Stephen's Hospital and my father called by to tell me he had died.

Elsaesser and her colleagues are continuing this long-term research project. However, the results of the first survey and numerous testimonies—including several ADCs similar to those I have experienced—were published in Elsaesser's book, *Spontaneous Contacts with the Deceased*. Their data will shed further light on ADCs and provide insights into their nature and purpose.

I don't know why I used to have so many paranormal experiences, but I am sure these are far more common than recognised. People seem reluctant to talk about it, perhaps for fear of being ostracised. I am hopeful that this book might be a catalyst for change, inspiring more open discussion and understanding.

As for me, having felt a profound loneliness of the soul my entire life, I suspect my mediumship might be related to living alone. My abilities increased at the onset of menopause and again whilst training as a spiritual healer and participating in my fortnightly meditation group, only to disappear when my mother's failing health brought her to live with me. Unsurprisingly, combining a full-time job with evening and weekend caretaking inevitably brought my fortnightly spiritual group meetings, freedom, and social life to an abrupt standstill.

If you're interested in exploring mediumship further, there are many excellent books on the subject. I highly recommend *The Afterlife Frequency: The Scientific Proof of Spiritual Contact and How That Awareness Will Change Your Life* by Mark Anthony, in which the Oxford-educated trial attorney coins the term "electromagnetic soul," noting that we are all just energy that never truly dies. I think he's right.

Future Memories—Can our Consciousness Flip to the Future?

Three examples I have described of what I call "consciousness flips" are when I predicted the demise of my Latin teacher when I was a teenager, then the death of a colleague decades later, and the coffee stain on the bedsheets when my medium chum Angie Kruger visited. Is there an explanation of how such premonitions may occur?

Many theoretical physicists, including Einstein, consider time an illusion created by the brain. Some postulate that we live in a block universe where the past, present, and future are one. I don't understand it since I am not mathematically minded. Still, it seems plausible, given that a Google search reveals that many people have had well-documented premonitions.

In a recent study, Dean Radin, Chief Scientist at the Institute of Noetic Sciences, postulated that our collective consciousness may be able to sense future events and that this may positively or negatively affect our mood in the present time. He looked at the emotional tone of Tweets over 13 years in ten languages and devised a "happiness score" related to words used, e.g., "Love" had a high score and "Terrorist" a low one.[*] The scores were then associated with subsequent significant international events. His results showed a definite downward trend in sentiment two weeks before an adverse event. Radin posited "that consciousness could be a fundamental element of the universe, akin to space and time. Such insights encourage us to rethink our position in the cosmos and contemplate the relationship between our thoughts and emotions and the world around us." Scary stuff!

As for me, I know that my consciousness has occasionally flipped to the future, and, as the saying goes, it only takes one black swan to prove that not all swans are white. Since I have seen a handful of "black swans," I know that future-flipping does exist, though I don't know how it happens or how to control it.

If you are interested in reading about more experiences of this nature, Teresa Cheung and Julia Mossbridge's *The Premonition Code* and

---

[*] https://www.tandfonline.com/eprint/IZQEGP8JYFMFG5YAQ2PP/full?target=10.1080/02604027.2023.2216629

PMH Atwater's *Future Memory* are good introductions. Many interesting presentations are also available on YouTube.

Can our Pets Communicate After Death?

I *know* that it's not just angels who help us. I've heard many stories of people's late pets communicating with them and helping them in certain circumstances. I had such an experience myself when my beloved Jack Russell, Fido, died unexpectedly in 2022, leaving me utterly bereft.

Some weeks later, having been unable to locate a Fido look-alike rescue dog, I bought a lifesaving Jack Russell puppy I named Jasper. An energetic little escape artist who is forever trying to break through the fenced boundaries of my large garden into my adjoining field to hunt whatever moves, Jasper's antics constantly keep me alert and on my toes. Nonetheless, I was surprised when, out of the blue one day, my medium friend Jane called to say that she had received a visual message from Fido, who seemed to be acting as some kind of protective guardian for my eleven-month-old puppy, which revealed that Jasper was escaping by chewing through the chicken wire fencing. Of course, I immediately checked the fences but found no way Jasper could escape. However, such is my faith in Jane that I continued checking for breaches daily until I eventually resigned myself to believing that her telepathic message from Fido was wrong.

But, of course, she wasn't. Some days later, when I thought Jasper was out foraging in the enclosed garden, I was suddenly alerted by an eerie silence. Jasper has jingle bells on his collar. I could always hear him. Now, suddenly, I couldn't hear anything. So where was he?

I poked around all the nooks and crannies. I climbed behind bushes and fallen tree trunks, calling Jasper's name in the hope that the bells would make sufficient noise for me to locate him. Eventually, after several heart-in-my-mouth minutes of frantic searching, I found Jasper sitting behind a tree, right next to a part of the grass-covered fence that had rusted and broken, with a guilty look on his face, as if to say, "It wasn't me. I didn't chew that hole in the fence."

I made a temporary repair with some chicken wire. Then I left a frustrated Jasper lamenting his foiled escape whilst I hurried off to get some extra strong welded mesh. I returned within minutes to find that Jasper had already made an even larger hole and was now stuck halfway through the fence, foiled from a complete getaway by a stray loop of chicken wire that had somehow managed to wrap itself around his willy. Luckily, I made a breech delivery, and Jasper was safe again. When I called Jane later to relay the tale, she pre-empted my story by describing the detailed image she had received from Fido, which was identical to what had actually happened.

That incident also begs the thought-provoking question: Can our late loved ones, both human and animal, actually see the future and give us warnings? If they can, it would shed doubt on whether everything is predetermined and whether the concept of free will is a delusion.

I often wonder how common it is for late pets to intervene to help an owner's new pet. Perhaps I am just lucky to have such spiritually gifted friends. But if you know of any stories like these, please share them with me.

This leads to my next chapter on what I *believe* but do not actually *know*.

CHAPTER 13

What I *Know* Vs. What I *Believe* About the Paranormal

Part Two: What I *Believe* But do Not (as Yet) *Know* is True

- Are Near-Death Experiences real?
- Do we have past lives?
- Do we have a predetermined life contract?
- Do we have free will?

Are Near-Death Experiences Real?

The term "near-Death Experiences" (NDEs) was first coined in 1975 by Dr Raymond Moody in his seminal book *Life After Life—The Investigation of a Phenomenon—Survival of Bodily Death*. I still have my original 49-year-old yellowed copy of Dr Moody's book, published the same year I qualified as a doctor.

I have read many books about NDEs but Dr Moody's book is a gem since it eloquently describes the essentials of NDEs: going through a tunnel with light at the end, meeting dead relatives, friends and pets, speaking to divine beings, having a life review, being aware of events away from the "deathbed," etc. *Life After Life* comprises numerous NDE case studies, and Dr Moody describes several where the NDE included a life review that initiated deep reflection and positive lifestyle changes. The section I find most interesting is entitled "Parallels," in which Dr Moody looks at historical evidence of the phenomenon, including the writings of the Greek philosopher Plato (428-348BC), who described experiences very similar to those included in *Life After Life*. He further adds: "Plato discusses in various passages how the soul which has been separated from the body may meet and converse with the departed Spirits of others and be guided through the transition from physical life to the next realm by guardian Spirits."

Moody also reveals that descriptions of NDEs are included in The Bible and the *Tibetan Book of Living and Dying*, and concludes: "It must be acknowledged that the existence of similarities and parallels among the writings of ancient thinkers and the reports of modern Americans who survive close brushes with death, remains a striking, and, so far, not definitively explicable fact."

Since the publication of *Life After Life*, many other academics have studied the NDE phenomenon, and numerous books are available for more in-depth reading.*

What I find most compelling, as noted by Mark Anthony in *The Afterlife Frequency*, is the similarity of NDEs in people from different countries and religions. Neither gender, race nor previous belief in the afterlife alter the classic NDE characteristics.

---

* These include *The Wisdom of Near Death Experiences: How Understanding NDEs Can Help Us to Live More Fully*, written by my friend and former colleague, Dr Penny Sartori; *After: a Doctor Explores What Near Death Experiences Reveal About Life and Beyond*, by Bruce Greyson; *Consciousness Beyond Life* by Pim van Lommel; *The Big Book of Near Death Experiences: The Ultimate Guide to the NDE and its After Effects* by PMH Atwater; *The Truth in the Light: An Investigation of Over 300 Near Death Experiences* by Peter Fenwick, and, my personal favourite, *The Afterlife Frequency—The Scientific Proof of Spiritual Contact and How That Awareness Will Change Your Life* by Mark Anthony.

Further evidence for NDEs as a genuine phenomenon is Shared Death Experiences (SDEs). As Mark Anthony notes in his book, "Sceptics have labelled NDEs as subjective since the account is based on one person's experience. SDEs, on the other hand, are objective since more than one person is involved during the experience." Mark Anthony references an article titled, "A Group of Firefighters' Near Death Experience," posted on September 20th, 2019, on the website www.near-death.com by Kevin Williams. In it, Williams describes events documented by the late NDE researcher Arvin Gibson. Williams' article is very detailed and worth reading, but here's a summary.

According to Williams, Arvin Gibson interviewed firefighter John Hernandez, crew boss for a group of 40 elite firefighters called Hotshots. In 1989, the Hotshots were dropped by helicopter onto a fire atop a mountain. Whilst preparing a fire break, which involved clearing and burning off combustible material, the wind changed, and the firefighters became trapped.

"One by one, the men and women fell to the earth suffocating from lack of oxygen," Hernandez said. Eventually, Hernandez found himself floating above his body, where he saw several of his crew members who were also floating in the air, including one crew member called Jose, who had a congenital foot deformity, which had now disappeared. On seeing this, Hernandez apparently looked at Jose and said: "Look, Jose, your foot is straight." Hernandez described how he also saw many late relatives, friends, pets, and, notably, his grandfather, who first appeared to Hernandez as an older man so that he would be recognised, and then later as a much younger man.

Williams's article provides many fascinating details, but the entire crew, all of whom reported some type of NDE, miraculously survived. Their reports were very similar, including observing Jose's normal foot, communicating with the Spirits of the other Hotshots, seeing a bright light, dead loved ones, and being given the choice to return.

As mentioned in Chapter Eight, in her book, *The Wisdom of Near-Death Experiences*, Dr Penny Sartori describes a man who experienced a partial resolution of a congenital deformity of his right hand following an NDE. Penny wrote: "This should not be physiologically possible as the tendons are in a permanently contracted position, so there is, as yet, no known mechanism to explain this aspect." The same goes for the firefighter whose foot deformity disappeared during his shared NDE, which leads me to wonder whether, in the afterlife, our entelechy or, as Mark Anthony terms it, "our electromagnetic soul," reverts to a perfect form.

As previously noted, when I suffered an adverse reaction to an antiemetic in 1975, I believe I may have experienced a partial NDE. I can still recall being semiconscious and very short of breath. Contrary to classical NDEs, I had no visions of a tunnel, dead relatives or bright lights. But I was aware of a benevolent being who offered me the choice of dying or returning. Since I was worried about my mum's mental state if I died, I chose to return.

Of course, this experience could have been caused by the effects of the drug, partial anoxia, or even just my imagination, so I cannot include NDEs in my *know* category. Still, the evidence for the veracity of NDEs is, to my mind, overwhelming—it's just that as a scientist, albeit a wannabe mystic scientist—I must engage my scientific training by putting it in the *believe* rather than the *know* category.

Do I believe NDEs are real? Before I answer that question, I first want to make clear that, despite how some of my stories might come across, my academic background and training did an excellent job of hard-wiring my brain in conventional practice and, hence, I am not easily persuaded by the experiences, publications, research, and beliefs of others. With that said, I do believe that NDEs are almost certainly an earthly preview of the afterlife, but, at present, no one can be sure of what actually happens after death. Maybe one day I can posthumously write a postscript on this, but meanwhile, here's two more critical questions: If physical death is not the end of our consciousness, what happened before our stint at Earth school? And what will happen after it?

Do we Have Past Lives?

I have no tangible evidence of my own past lives and have never had a past-life regression session or a complete NDE. However many credible authors have since published books about NDEs, pre-life contracts, and other people's past life experiences. Hence, I believe the following is possibly—and even probably—true.

One of my favourite books about past lives is Tom Shroder's *Old Souls*, in which he describes the work of Dr Ian Stevenson, whose research into past lives spanned almost four decades and comprises over 2,000 cases. Shroder, a respected journalist and writer, was privileged to accompany Dr Stevenson in some of his fieldwork. In this book, he details many of Stevenson's cases. One that caught my attention was the reincarnation story of a Lebanese woman called Suzanne Ghanem, born on 21st March, 1972, in a suburb of Beirut.

Suzanne's parents were of the monotheistic Druze faith, the followers of which believe in reincarnation. A very early speaker, Suzanne insisted from a very young age that her real name was Saada Hatoum, who, it transpired, had died on 11th March 1972. Suzanne claimed that Saada had a daughter called Leila and a husband named Halim. She could also identify 23 family members from that past life and document their correct relationships with Saada. Suzanne's parents eventually took her to visit Saada's family. Once there, Suzanne gave further details of her life as Saada, including a correct telephone number with just the last two digits reversed. Shroder's book contains more remarkable information, including comparable photographs of Saada and Suzanne at similar ages.

Shroder noted that the Arabic word for "reincarnation" is *takamous*, which means "changing your shirt," and that "the Druze believe that the body is just clothes for the soul, and that when you are reincarnated, it is like changing your clothes." Shroder also noted that the Arabian word for reincarnated boys is *natiq*, and for girls, *natak*. According to Shroder, both these words translate to "one who talks about past lives."

The idea of our body being our metaphysical clothing is a comforting analogy. However, I believe that our body is simply a temporary vessel for the soul that eventually becomes worn out, freeing us for our next adventure.

Whilst many excellent books on past lives explore the concept in detail, I would recommend Brian Weiss's series on past life regression, which is very readable and informative. According to Weiss, some people who have had past life regression analysis note that paying for karmic debts accrued in a past life is an integral part of pre-life planning. It seems logical that if we have caused harm in one life, then we should atone for it in the next, and this is a recurring theme in Weiss's series. I have no personal experience to validate this belief except for two unusual incidents:

The first was during a female genitourinary medicine clinic when I was a young and remarkably naïve junior doctor working at the Middlesex Hospital in London in 1976. One of my patients was a beautiful and very experienced bubbly prostitute. We had an instant rapport, and during the interview, I had to ask her about her work practices to assess her risk of sexually acquired infection and to target specific anatomical sites which would need screening.

The lady was reluctant to give details, but I intuitively knew what her bizarre niche prostitute work involved and could relate this to her. She immediately giggled and told me that to know what I had told her, I must have been a high-class prostitute before working as a doctor. To this day, I can still remember her laughter and absolute conviction that I had been a prostitute. In fact, I had never received any teaching on such matters and had no idea where my information had come from

The second weird incident, which may shed some light on this anomaly, occurred several decades later when I was a consultant in Swansea. It's a strange tale involving a one-inch bronze Roman pendant in the shape of male external genitalia, known as a *fascinus*. I had found the pendant in an antique shop in Caldicott near where I lived. It was locked in a glass cabinet, and maybe because I spent my working week examining the living versions, I thought the tiny erect penis was rather cute and I had to buy it. I learned that it was almost 2,000 years old and was worn to evoke the Roman God Fascinus to ward off the evil eye and provide protection, particularly for children and soldiers.

Several months later, I took the pendant to a spiritual development workshop run by a nationally famous medium. We had been told to bring an object for a psychometry session. During the session, the course leader said that my *fascinus* had belonged to me in a former life when I had been a prostitute in ancient Rome. Apparently, I was wearing it when I died in a gutter, ravaged by sexually transmitted infection.

Naturally, I would have preferred a more glamorous past life. Still, if this reading was accurate, it would certainly explain why having doubtless spread a lot of sexually transmitted diseases in that past life, I have not only been largely abstinent in this life but also have treated thousands of such infections. It would also confirm Brian Weiss's ideas that the negative karma we build up in one life must eventually be balanced. The jury is out as to whether I believe that, but it is a cool story, and given that I was named after a Roman goddess, I like to think there might be a link somewhere.

Another reason why I *believe*, but do not yet *know* for sure, that past lives exist is my strange connection with blue star energy. Despite having little first-hand evidence of my past lives, I have had several inexplicable experiences involving blue star energy and an apparent past life as a blue star priestess. If I'd had just one experience, it would be easy to shrug off. However, having had many similar experiences at different times and in other locations, all of which were confirmed by several people, it's not so easy to ignore.

As referenced in Chapter Six, my first blue star connection occurred in 2003. My second experience occurred three years later in July 2006, when I attended a three-day healing fair. I was wandering around a large, crowded marquee like a child in Santa's grotto, entranced by the many bright stalls selling everything from crystals, drums, incense, and shamanic artefacts to sessions with palm readers, handwriting analysts, mediums, and Reiki and Bach Flower Remedy practitioners, when my attention was caught by a jewellery stall run by a couple with a shop in Glastonbury. I was waiting politely at the back of a crowd of women jostling one another to get to the front of the stall when, suddenly, the stallholder left her position, walked towards me at the back of the crowd and without introduction, announced, "I see you are from Sirius. Would you mind coming outside with me so I can connect with blue star energy and visit home?"

Initially baffled by the ludicrousness of the stranger's request but secretly hoping that something magical might be in store, I meekly complied. Once outside the tent, the lady held both her hands about six to nine inches above mine with our palms facing for several seconds, and then thanked me and went back to her stall. I hadn't felt a thing, and over time, came to dismiss the encounter as another inexplicable but possible past life link with Sirius. I never saw the stall holder again and likely would have forgotten all about it… if it hadn't been for her references to blue star energy and Sirius, both of which seemed to be cropping up with increasing frequency around that time.

Another blue star-related incident occurred on the day that I received angelic healing from Sharon at the 2006 trance workshop that I wrote about in Chapter Six. Following my session with Sharon, I was approached by Paul, an older man who asked me in broken English to sit and have coffee with him. Since he seemed highly agitated, I agreed. With tears in his eyes, Paul said he had seen blue light above my head and knew it meant I could heal him. Surprised but touched by his obvious distress, I took his hands in mine and gently transmitted healing energy to him. I have no idea what ailed Paul, but after I held his hands and prayed, he calmed down, and we rejoined the workshop. Later that same day, another woman in our group approached me and asked if I knew I had been a blue star priestess in a past life!

As if that weren't enough, I had yet another blue star encounter the following year when I was in Scotland attending a three-day workshop led by medical intuitive and author Caroline Myss. The workshop was based on her book *Entering the Castle—Finding the Inner Path to God and Your Soul's Purpose*, which was about St. Teresa of Avila.

It was the first evening of the event. We were gathered in the beautifully appointed Kintyre room at what was then known as The

Westin Turnberry Hotel in Ayrshire. The hotel was very posh, and the Kintyre room looked radiant with its elegantly dressed and laid tables, glittering chandeliers, and walls covered with photographs of previous guests—including the former American president Jimmy Carter and many other dignitaries—that I felt way out of my comfort zone. So, I had resorted to dressing in my day job consultant armour: a smart suit in muted colours.

I was hungry, so I arrived early for our evening meal. I sat at an empty table and was soon joined by a well-dressed older lady who introduced herself as Liz and told me that having scanned the room, she felt I was the only person she resonated with. I soon learned that Liz lived in Jersey and was training with the medical anthropologist Alberto Villoldo. Coincidentally, I had just read Alberto's book, *Shaman, Healer, Sage*, and was enthralled by his wisdom, so I was delighted to have such an informed dinner companion.

We were chatting about Liz's mentor over dinner when she suddenly fell silent, gazed deeply into my eyes, and boldly declared, "We have had past lives together, and we were both blue star priestesses at the Temple of Isis in Philae." Having heard this before, I wasn't particularly shocked. But the fact that we were at such a magical venue, and Liz looked so very normal, somehow made her statement hit home. So I told her of an experience I'd had a few months previously with a friend who was a highly educated IT project manager and a gifted medium, during which my friend and I had somehow metaphysically mind-melded and spontaneously regressed to a past life in which I was her mother. We were both blue star priestesses at the temple of Isis in Philae, where we were in charge of a library in which all the information was stored in crystals, not books. Liz confirmed that this was indeed how books were stored at that time.

Several months later, I attended another Mind Body Spirit event at a local hotel, which, despite having a decent number of stalls selling crystals, incense, and other new-age artefacts, didn't seem to have attracted much of a crowd. Several mediums were in attendance, and after wandering around for a bit, I settled on one particularly forlorn-looking woman called Karen, whose stall was laid out with models of Egyptian gods and goddesses and several well-used tarot decks.

Karen was a lovely lady with a bubbly, exuberant personality. As I patiently waited while she entered a semi-trance state, I had no idea she was about to blow my mind. Then, to my surprise, she suddenly said, "'You are one of the few to teach the many, and your soul's name is Blue Star Diamond." I was lost for words. I could pass off one or two references to blue stars as a coincidence but it had now been mentioned by more than half a dozen individuals, none of whom knew me or each other. What on earth was going on? I was still none the wiser.

After that encounter, I heard nothing more about blue stars and my connection to them until recently, when my friend Jennifer invited her spiritually sensitive medical colleague Debbie to my house for coffee. Whilst conversing about current medical practice, Debbie suddenly turned to me and said, "Do you know you have a blue light above your head?" Neither of them knew about my blue star connection. So, once again, it was a complete mystery. My colourful stalker had returned, but I still had no idea what it meant.

Do we Have a Predetermined Life Contract?

The existence of a pre-life contract is almost a universal dogma in countless books on spiritual philosophy, including those of Dolores Cannon and one of my favourites, *Your Soul's Plan* by Robert Schwartz. The general consensus seems to be that when we die, we meet departed family, friends, and pets and then have a life review during which we get to see all the events in our life and get to viscerally "experience" both the pain and the pleasure that we were responsible for causing others. There is no judgment. Having the opportunity to experience the feelings our actions caused is sufficient for us to learn the lesson of "do unto others as you would have them do unto you." Then, with the help of our Spirit guides, or possibly angels, we may have the opportunity to reincarnate. From what I have read, it seems we have a team of people/spiritual beings/guides, etc., who help us choose our next life, the archetypal patterns needed to support the lessons we have to learn, and the people who will reincarnate with us to ensure our new pre-life contract is fulfilled. Apparently, we even get to choose our parents, but before we slip into our mother's womb, all is forgotten.

Crazy, eh? But is there any evidence to support any of these metaphysical concepts?

Regardless of whether any of the above is true, some of the ideas these concepts generate have practical implications in the real world. For example, the Swiss psychiatrist and founder of analytical psychology, Carl Jung believed that we are all born with archetypal patterns of behaviour that exist in our collective unconscious. Jung identified four main archetypes (archetype means "original pattern" in ancient Greek) within all humans. These are The Persona, The Shadow, The Anima or

Animus, and The Self. Jung further defined twelve other archetypes: The Innocent, The Orphan, The Hero, The Caregiver, The Explorer, The Rebel, The Lover, The Creator, The Jester, The Sage, The Magician, and The Ruler. Caroline Myss has developed her own more complex take on archetypal patterns which resonates more closely with my beliefs.

Myss believes we are all born with twelve support archetypes, of which four are universal: The Victim, The Prostitute, The Saboteur, and The Child. Myss considers that these innate archetypes help determine our behaviour and aid in completing our life's purpose, our "sacred contract." Myss has many free videos concerning archetypal patterns on her website at https://Myss.com, and her book, *Sacred Contracts: Awakening your Divine Potential* elegantly describes what a sacred contract is and how to determine your own. Published in 2003, I regard this book as a "must read" for anyone who wants to know, "Why am I here, and what is my life's purpose?"

Caroline Myss has also produced a set of archetype cards aimed at helping us recognise our own and other people's archetypes. Each card shows the light (typically positive) and shadow (generally negative) characteristics of a specific archetype, which offers a helpful introduction to the concept. As an example, Myss's "The Story Teller's" card describes the "light" aspect as the ability to experience and express life through stories and symbols, whilst the shadow aspect makes up tales that harm others. Many politicians have this archetype!

I developed an exercise using Myss's archetype cards for a workshop held at the postgraduate centre in Abergavenny in 2014 to teach local trainee GPs about the importance of understanding their own and their patients' archetypes.

If we have specific predetermined archetypes, they must exist as energy forms in our consciousness and probably also in the auric field around our body. In the workshop, I asked the doctors to look carefully at the cards, read the brief descriptions of the archetypes' light and shadow attributes, and list those they thought they had. They then paired up with someone they least knew and held hands with each other whilst imagining they were breathing into their partner's heart. This was done for three deep breaths, after which they wrote down the archetypes they felt their partners had. In retrospect, they were carrying out psychometry on each other.

Finally, I asked the doctors to gauge the concordance between their assessment of their personal archetypes and their partners. After this, we had a group discussion, and although we did not have time to analyse the data, most seemed intrigued by the degree of concordance. Several admitted they had discovered aspects of themselves of which they had not previously been aware.

All healthcare workers, and indeed every individual, would benefit from being taught Jungian/Myss archetypal patterns at school, let alone just medical/nursing school. An intimate understanding of our own and others' innate patterns could lead to greater empathy, fewer arguments, and less stress-induced illness. It's important to recognise, nurture, and positively relate to one's specific archetypes and to learn when things may go badly because of falling into the shadow. Trying to act out an archetype you don't have also could end in tears.

The older I've become, the more I have developed my innate eccentric hedge witch archetype. I prefer to dress in comfy, decades-old clothes and commune mostly with my dog and Nature. The rare occasions I have to dress up for excursions into normalcy are stressful since I don't have a fashionista archetype and resolutely try to avoid wearing a claustrophobic bra.

Occasionally, I have even developed stress/immune-related illnesses to avoid the stressor, including gut problems, cardiac arrythmias, and common colds. On one occasion, whilst working as a very junior registrar, I awoke with a sudden complete loss of voice on a day when I was supposed to give a lecture at Queen Charlotte's Hospital. Terrified that I would collapse with nerves, I had literally become speechless. Realising my body was responding to my fear of public speaking, I gently thanked it for giving me an appropriate "get out of jail card" but also said I really needed to overcome this irrational fear. After a few hours, my voice returned, the lecture went well, and I discovered that Public Speaker and Teacher are two of the more developed archetypes that have served me well in my career, especially when I once had to address some two thousand doctors at an international meeting.

I intuitively learned to work with archetypes before discovering Jung's/Myss's teachings. But sometimes, even with this knowledge, we are forced by circumstance into adopting an archetypal pattern that drains our souls. Such was my experience when I was forced to adopt the archetype of the "Indentured Servant."

Given the lack and cost of social care and the rising numbers of elderly people needing support, many are finding themselves becoming long term (and often very reluctant) indentured servants when taking care of elderly relatives. Being forced to give up work, friends, holidays, etc., can quickly turn our lives into a joyless and overwhelming wilderness of despair.

I survived my own prolonged indentured servitude to my mother. Although I sometimes did not like my mum, I did love her. But when she was particularly aggressive, I often prayed and asked for the grace to survive the moment. When the indenture inevitably ended, that alien archetype had become such a large part of my life that I felt as if I was an egg whose entire contents had been sucked dry. Anxiety, panic attacks, and shaking were just some of the symptoms that beset me as a result of the years of prolonged stress, culminating in a collapse.

My doctor prescribed an antidepressant, a serotonin reuptake inhibitor (SSI), which made my anxiety unbearably worse. Although some people do benefit from these drugs, one size does not fit all, and I had to stop taking them after three days. I turned to alternative approaches, like swimming, regular reflexology sessions, and Indian head massages, which helped me cope with severe panic attacks. Even so, I did collapse on one occasion and ended up in a cardiac ward with what my doctor diagnosed as "broken heart syndrome." Such is the consequence of living with a non-innate archetype!

To end this section on pre-determined life contracts and archetypes, I must mention how positive and joyful it is to discover and fully embrace one's main archetypal patterns. I have a lifelong Writer archetype, plus the Teacher, Gardener, Cook, Dog lover, and Clown. For me, waking up with my little dog asleep on top of my head, talking to my tomato and runner bean plants before breakfast, cooking a meal for a friend, and an evening of writing constitute the perfect day.

My only additional personal experience in supporting pre-life contracts is a single numerology reading I had with Michaela Wynn-Jones, which, despite my initial scepticism, was so accurate I felt as if she had been sitting on my shoulder my entire life. Michaela told me I was destined to be a writer but could also be a healer and an academic doctor. If pre-life contracts are a myth, then I question how Michaela could tell me so much about my life's path merely from knowing my name and date of birth. Perhaps our names and birth dates are linked to our souls' Akashic records, in which case the concept of pre-life sacred contracts does make sense.

Do we Have Free Will?

The short answer is No, and, Yes, depending on which side of life you happen to be.

For a long time, it has disturbed me that most spiritual teachers feel we have free will, are directly responsible for our actions, and have a choice. I don't feel this is the case on this side of the veil, at least in the broad outline of our lives and significant life events and relationships. Maybe we can choose which flavour of ice cream to order, but I don't believe we have many choices over what careers we pursue, where we live, who we meet, who we significantly interact with, whether we have children, etc.

Since childhood, I have felt I saw the world differently from my peers. I preferred my own company communicating with wildlife, bees, birds, trees, my Spirit friend and the like, rather than going to teenage social gatherings. I cannot recall going to a single dance when I was a teenager and was surprised when, on recently speaking to some old school friends who were "normal," I discovered just how atypical I was. When my peers were enamoured with The Beatles, I would be reading books such as *Albert Einstein: The Man and His Theories* by Hilare Cuny, which I acquired in 1965 and still possess.

Whilst I have on several occasions tried to emulate my happily married peers by attempting a Stepford wife role, at heart, I know I was always destined to be alone. I suspect this is also part of my sacred contract since it may be harder to hear the still, small voice of Spirit if one is part of a family group. Also, in my case, the internationally recognised medical research I did was so time-consuming it would not have been possible if I'd had family commitments. Whilst I cannot say it has been an entirely joyful life, I have few regrets since I feel sure it was a life agreed to before incarnating, and I do have good friends and a dog!

So, in brief, I do not believe we have free will in this life. And I was intrigued to read that much greater minds have felt the same, including my teenage heartthrob, Albert Einstein, who, in an interview with George Viereck published in The Saturday Evening Post on October 26th, 1929, made the following comments:

"I am a determinist. As such, I do not believe in free will. The Jews believe in free will. They believe that man shapes his own life. I reject that doctrine philosophically. In that respect I am not a Jew… I believe with Schopenhauer: We can do what we wish, but we can only wish what we must. Practically, I am, nevertheless, compelled to act as if freedom of the will existed. If I wish to live in a civilized community, I must act as if man is a responsible being."

"I know that philosophically, a murderer is not responsible for his crime; nevertheless, I must protect myself from unpleasant contacts."

"My own career was undoubtedly determined, not by my own will but by various factors over which I have no control—primarily those mysterious glands in which Nature prepares the very essence of our life, our internal secretions… Socrates referred to it as his Daimon… Each explains in his own way the undeniable fact that the human will is not free."

"I claim credit for nothing. Everything is determined, the beginning as well as the end, by forces over which we have no control. It is determined for the insect as well as for the star. Human being, vegetables or cosmic dust, we all dance to an invisible tune, intoned in the distance by a mysterious player."

I believe Einstein nailed it regarding free will. But although I don't believe we truly have free will once we have incarnated, I do believe that when we plan our lives, we are allowed choices, which are a form of free will. However, once we agree to our sacred contract, I suspect we must accept the apparent "slings and arrows of outrageous fortune."

PART 4

THROUGH THE LOOKING GLASS

CHAPTER 14

Global Chaos, the Paranormal, and the Concept of Wetiko

Our world has become increasingly chaotic. The emotional, physical and economic aftermath of the pandemic, the Ukraine/Russia and Israel/Gaza wars, climate change, energy crises, and natural disasters have made fear of the future part of the fabric of our everyday lives. The rate of change since the COVID-19 pandemic has been overwhelming, and, living in the internet era, we can see not only local problems but also the effects of war and climate change in real-time. Other people's suffering is seen in graphic, soul-destroying detail and has become the central issue of our news.

Many of us wonder if there is a loving God when it seems that millions are just born to suffer and to create children who also suffer before dying frequently painful deaths. The masses often endure severe hardships whilst the wealthy are insulated from most of life's economic problems, jetting off to foreign climes whilst the poor shiver in their hovels. It is heartbreaking to see that recent global events have set many people back into a level of poverty that we have not known since my mother's generation were children.

My mother, born in 1920, was the daughter of Emlyn, a coal miner who fought in the front line in the trenches in Ypres. She frequently saw my grandfather shed tears over what he had experienced. She told me that when Emlyn returned from the war, little work was available in the Welsh valleys. The local coal mine owner would send his foreman out with a horse and cart and throw shovels to the waiting men. Only those who could fight for a shovel got employed for a day's work. My mum and her sister often had to share a single boiled egg—the only protein sometimes available in their tiny Welsh cottage. However, they were religious (Welsh Wesleyans), and anarchy did not prevail. Indeed, Emlyn became a much sought-after lay preacher renowned for his *hwyl* (passionate/ecstatic Welsh preaching). The Church and the State certainly controlled the family.

Mum always said that working-class people should not have children because they are just gun fodder for the ruling classes. 'So why did you have me?' I once asked. She apologised, saying that she was in love with my dad and that having children was what the Church and society expected of married couples.

In existential times, many people receive great solace from their religious beliefs. But others, like me, wonder if many orthodox religions actually serve the needs of the individual or merely allow the state to control the masses by manipulating behaviour through fear of divine retribution. Voltaire famously encapsulated this concept when he said, "There is no God, but don't tell that to my servant, lest he murder me at night." Indeed, Yuval Harari, in his book *Sapiens*, explains how up to 150 people can co-exist in a community by simply having intimate knowledge of each other. However, when this number is exceeded, chaos may prevail unless the group has common myths that exist only in people's imagination. He notes that these myths may relate to religion, statehood, and judicial systems.

Sadly, many of the world's great religions have evolved into institutions where religious leaders exert their authority over the population in the name of whatever prophet or God they align with. In particular, women are often seen as men's property and denied equal rights. If we each have a direct connection with God, Universal Consciousness, Spirit, etc., earthly intermediaries such as priests, mullahs, and rabbis would be redundant. No one likes to have their power taken away, and heresy is severely punished in many cultures. The current religious oppression of women in theocracies and increasingly overtly Western democracies makes it all too clear how religion can be used to control the population. Women, especially, are often further controlled regarding education, permitted dress, birth control, legal rights, etc. In the long term, however, with virtually universal access to mobile phones, women will be more able to communicate with each other, and this global oppression may eventually end. But, I fear, not without the loss of many lives and much personal sacrifice.

Throughout my medical career, I have intimately observed the physical and mental suffering of countless others. These include patients with AIDS who, before antiviral therapy was available, often had hideous and heart-rending deaths, trauma victims of terrorist attacks, children and adults with terminal cancers, including many close friends and family members, rape victims, and survivors of sexual abuse. I sometimes literally felt their pain in a specific region of my body that correlated with the location of their pain, and I still find it very stressful being in groups where the collective energy is at odds with mine. You don't have to be an extreme empath to sense negative energy.

If we know what may be going on energetically at a global level, we can do our best to moderate its negative effects. This is particularly crucial in these times when the likelihood of nuclear war is higher than it has been since the Cuban crisis in October 1962, when I was thirteen. I can still recall the fear we had of imminent nuclear war and the futile duck-and-dive instructions we were given at school. Now, global self-destructive madness is again threatening our existence. I am sure that ordinary folks working hard to support their families don't really want to be involved with the politics of greed and fear that lead to wars. But, somehow, we do get involved, take sides, and in the main, follow the lead of our governments. So, what is going on in our collective subconscious? This is where the concept of wetiko may shine some light.

What is Wetiko?

Paul Levy is a thought leader in spiritual development. A Tibetan Buddhist practitioner, artist, writer and expert on wetiko, his books describe the concept, its local and global effects, and how to weaken its power. *In Wetiko: Healing the Mind-Virus that Plagues Our World*, Paul Levy notes:

> "A contagious, psycho-spiritual disease of the soul, a parasite of the mind, is currently being acted out en masse on the world stage, via an insidious collective psychosis of titanic proportions. This mind virus—which the Native Americans have called 'wetiko' covertly operates through the unconscious blind spots in the human psyche, rendering people oblivious to their own madness and compelling them to act against their own best interests. Wetiko is a psychosis in the true sense of the word, a sickness of the spirit."

Wetiko is a challenging concept to grasp. But from what I understand, it may explain why the world is currently in a state of increasing chaos and, hence, is worthy of discussion.

An article by Ladha and Kirk published in Kosmos Journal, Spring/Summer, 2016, entitled "Seeing Wetiko: On Capitalism, Mind, and

Antidotes for a World in Transition," gives a comprehensive and insightful description of wetiko. Ladha and Kirk explain that wetiko is a Native American term for a metaphysical archetype of "a cannibalistic spirit driven by greed, excess, and selfish consumption." They add that "wetiko short-circuits an individual's ability to see itself as an enmeshed and interdependent part of a balanced environment and raises the self-serving ego to supremacy." It's part of what Jung called our collective universal subconscious. Native Americans considered wetiko a cannibalistic spirit (mind virus) that induces its host to steal the life force of other living creatures and is indifferent to its consequences. Ladha and Kirk argue that many of the traits of modern capitalism are manifestations of wetiko and that "those who live in a wetiko culture will manifest, to one degree or other, wetiko beliefs and behaviour."

Christmas is a time when it is easy to see how we are all programmed into a wetiko mindset from an early age. Children are generally oblivious to how peer pressure, social media, television, etc., encourage them to want more and more, even if their parents have to go hungry to provide it. I lament the seemingly universal materialistic madness that takes over each year, resulting in the earth's resources being further depleted and landfill sites being overwhelmed. It is sad, but it is wetiko incarnate.

So, what can be done to de-programme or de-wetiko-ise our consciousness?

Ladha and Kirk draw hope for change by linking the concept of wetiko with the science of epigenetics. They write:

"For those who prefer their science more empirical, the growing field of epigenetics provides some intellectual concrete. Epigenetics studies changes in organisms caused by modification of gene expression, rather than any physical alteration of the gene itself.

In other words, how traits vary from generation to generation is not solely a question of material biology, but is partly determined by environmental and contextual factors that affected our ancestors, and then are triggered within our genetic sequence through activation events in our life."

Epigenetics has become part of mainstream science, and one of its leading advocates, Dr Bruce Lipton, has written a best-selling book called *The Biology of Belief: Unleashing the Power of Consciousness, Matter & Miracles*. Lipton teaches that if we become aware of our toxic beliefs and resolve to un-programme our conscious mind, we can induce favourable gene expression and ultimately improve our health. Likewise, Ladha and Kirk propose that one of the starting points for healing is the simple act of "seeing wetiko in ourselves, in others, and in our social infrastructure." Once we are consciously aware of the wetiko "virus" and its toxic effects on us and the natural environment, we can weaken it. Ladha and Kirk say, "By contracting new relationships with others, with Nature, and ourselves, we can build a new complex of entanglements and thought-forms fused with post-wetiko, post-capitalistic values."

This is where wetiko links up with the work of Lynne McTaggart. I first came across McTaggart's work in 2002 when my sister mentioned her book *The Field* in a phone call. I read it in May of that year when I was at the very beginning of my spiritual awakening and was concerned that my sudden, albeit only occasional, ability to communicate with dead people may be psychotic. McTaggart discusses many "paranormal" phenomena in *The Field*, including homoeopathy, distant viewing, telepathy, mediumship, and the healing energy field. *The Field* saved my sanity since, at the time, my logical left brain needed reassurance that my paranormal experiences could probably be scientifically explained.

McTaggart's next book, *The Bond: Connecting Through the Space Between Us*, looks more deeply into the interconnectedness of everything and everyone. In the introduction, McTaggart aptly—albeit inadvertently— describes wetiko in action when she states, "In our relationships we extol our inherent right to individual happiness and self-expression above all else. We educate our young by encouraging them to compete and excel over their peers. The currency of most modern two-cars-in-every-garage neighbourhoods is comparison and one-upmanship." She later adds, "On a personal level, it [a materialistic view of life] has left most of us with a distinctly hollow feeling, as though something profound—our very humanity—has been trampled on in our daily wrestle with the world. We urgently need a new story to live by."

Published in 2011, *The Bond* is even more pertinent today. Over the past decade, we've witnessed an alarming dehumanisation of our lives. The closure of high street banks and Post Offices has deprived the less tech-savvy among us of essential services and human interaction. Automated supermarket checkouts and self-service petrol stations, often our only options, erode our interpersonal skills and the healing power of simple human contact. Our world is becoming increasingly lonely, particularly for the elderly and infirm, who may have limited social interactions. The isolation imposed by the pandemic has underscored our inherent need for human connection. I remember how during the Covid lockdown, even a brief, socially-distanced conversation with a masked grocery delivery man became the highlight of my week.

Technology and the wetiko "virus" that it helps transmit appears to have made our lives easier, but are we happier? Life was much simpler when, for example, cars ran only on one petrol grade and were paid for in cash to a friendly cashier who only sold petrol.

People need people, and social isolation, particularly in older generations, is a well-recognised risk factor for many diseases, including dementia, heart disease, stroke, depression, anxiety, and suicide. Equally, being part of a group with similar interests may counteract at least some of the adverse effects of our wetiko-ridden society. Eye-to-eye contact, I believe, links us to another person's soul and is sometimes healing in itself just because it says, "I care."

One way I used to teach medical students how to interact with patients was to ask a student to sit opposite me in a role-playing exercise and have them talk to me for precisely two minutes about their last holiday or why they wanted to be a doctor, etc. For the first minute, I would look at the student, nod my head, and be very attentive, and then in the final minute, I would avoid all eye contact, pretend to look at a PC monitor, yawn, tap my watch, etc. I would then ask the students to note their feelings during the attentive and inattentive periods. In one case, a student could only tolerate ten seconds of my ignoring her before blurting out, "I am sorry, Dr Blackwell, but I really want to kill you; I can't go on." It was a great response, and I asked her and the rest of the class to remember how this felt and be aware of how a patient may feel if you look at a monitor rather than into their eyes.

Sadly, since my teaching days, fewer people can see their doctors face to face anymore. With telephone consultations becoming the norm, we already see the effects of missed or late diagnoses and the total absence of the healing that can occur simply by being with your doctor. Although I have used a doctor-patient scenario here, the same applies to any social interaction: we need to connect with other people or risk our health and even our existence. This is where the formation of small, like-minded groups can help.

In 2003, I set up a group comprising mainly stressed-out consultants and nurses from my hospital, plus a few general practitioners, counsellors, a social worker, and occasional guests. Each session would include an opening prayer, a talking/sharing segment, and a guided meditation with relaxing drumming. By the end, everyone would feel pretty chilled. I would also bring along research papers on such matters as the healing power of prayer so that we could discuss and learn from each other's views.

In retrospect, I suspect the group energy allowed us to partially extract some of the manifestations of wetiko in our lives. I recall one of the senior doctors in the group telling me years later that she had only managed to get through one dreadfully stressful week by thinking about our next meeting.

Following her research study of the power of intention (AKA the power of prayer) and her books and online "Power of Eight" Intention Masterclasses, McTaggart has brought together thousands of people in "Power of Eight" intention groups that meet regularly in person or online to discuss their problems and set intentions for healing/resolution of whichever issues concern one or more of their members. She has also organised much larger intention experiments to help influence and hopefully resolve global problems, based on the premise that we are all connected at a quantum level and hence can use our collective consciousness to resolve existential worldwide issues. A way, perhaps, to free ourselves from our self-centred wetiko-induced global chaos?

I fervently hope so.

How Badly Affected by Wetiko are we?

In 2009, I came across a brilliant book by Professor Charles Tart called *The End of Materialism*, in which he introduces a concept called The Western Creed, which encapsulates the beliefs of modern Western society. In my view, his Creed is a present-day manifestation of wetiko. Tart says that he did not really create the Creed but "merely took beliefs that are widely held and taught over and over again in our culture, both explicitly and implicitly, and put them in a form like a religious creed to help make clearer the potential impacts of these beliefs." Tart gives instructions as to how to use the Creed and advises not to analyse it intellectually but "the point is to just do it and observe your emotional and bodily reactions."

I tried the Western Creed exercise myself and was intrigued by my responses. So, I decided to create a Spiritual Creed and see how some medical students reacted to both Creeds. I asked a volunteer to stand up and read the Western Creed out loud as if swearing an oath. My students were very bright graduate entry students with enquiring minds and although a few could read the Western Creed with no negative feelings, most disliked it to varying degrees. I particularly recall one bubbly female student who got as far as the third sentence and then turned towards me, saying, "I feel sick and am choking." Analogously, reading the Spiritual Creed had the opposite effect on most, who sensed no adverse impact on their emotional state or bodily sensations. As expected, the few students who coped well with the Western Creed did not resonate well with the Spiritual Creed.

I often wondered if Professor Tart's Creed exercise could be linked to those students' future medical/surgical speciality choices. Sadly, I only discovered Professor Tart's ideas shortly before I retired and could not pursue that enquiry. Hopefully, someone reading this may try out the exercise, and if they get the same reaction I did, then perhaps I will have sown a seed. I suspect one's response to both Creeds may link to how deeply wetiko is entrenched in one's consciousness.

The Western Creed

(From "*The End of Materialism*" by Charles Tart, copyright 2009 New Harbinger Publications, Inc. With permission)

I BELIEVE in the material universe as the only and ultimate reality, a universe controlled by fixed physical laws and blind chance.

I AFFIRM that the universe has no creator, no objective purpose, and no objective meaning or destiny.

I MAINTAIN that all ideas about God or gods, supernatural beings, prophets and saviors, or other nonphysical beings or forces are superstitions and delusions. Life and consciousness are totally identical to physical processes, and arose from chance interactions of blind physical forces. Like the rest of life, my life and consciousness have no objective purpose, meaning, or destiny.

I BELIEVE that all judgements, values, and moralities, whether my own or others', are subjective, arising solely from biological determinants, personal history, and chance. Free will is an illusion. Therefore, the most rational values I can personally live by must be based on the knowledge that for me what pleases me is Good, what pains me is Bad. Those who please me or help me avoid pain are my friends; those who pain me or keep me from my pleasures are my enemies. Rationality requires that friends and enemies be used in ways that maximize my pleasure and minimize my pain.

I AFFIRM that churches have no real use other than social support; that there are no objective sins to commit or be forgiven for; that there is no retribution for sin or reward for virtue other than that which I can arrange, directly or through others. Virtue for me is getting what I want without being caught and punished by others.

I MAINTAIN that the death of the body is the death of the mind. There is no afterlife, and all hope for such is nonsense.

A Spiritual Creed
(ALB)

I BELIEVE in both the material and energetic world, which is organised by both known physical laws and by as yet unidentified forces.

I AFFIRM that the universe has a creator with specific objectives and that all creation has meaning and destiny.

I MAINTAIN that ideas about God or gods, enlightened beings-prophets, and saviours, or other non-physical beings or forces are real entities. Life and consciousness comprise physical processes and energies we don't fully understand. All life arose from the universal energy field, and all life, including my life and my consciousness, has a specific purpose, meaning and destiny.

I BELIEVE that I have free will to determine what decisions I make in order to follow my divine purpose. People in my life are part of my sacred contract, and whether my interactions with them appear good or bad, they are part of my soul's journey, and I will learn from everyone I meet.

I AFFIRM that spiritual groups provide social and spiritual support, that like attracts like and that what you give out will eventually be reflected back to you.

I BELIEVE that death of the body does not cause the death of one's consciousness and that I will be reborn many times until I reach a state of enlightenment and can remain an energetic being of pure love.

I used to teach my students a kinesiology exercise to demonstrate how our conscious thoughts can affect our emotional and physical state. It involves asking a volunteer (preferably of a similar build to oneself) to stand beside you with their left arm extended out to the side. You then ask them to resist when you push down on their extended arm. This is their personal strength control exercise. You then repeat the procedure, but this time, ask the volunteer to repeatedly state a positive, true affirmation such as, "I love my dog, partner, work, etc., or even my name is⎯⎯⎯⎯⎯⎯"

When they do this, the strength in the extended arm usually remains unchanged from the control. The next step is to ask them to lie about something they feel very strongly about. When their arm is tested, their strength is often so weakened they are shocked.

I once conducted this experiment with a consultant neurologist to see if he could explain how it could occur. He happened to have a very marked reduction in strength when we carried out the third exercise, and he admitted both his surprise at what he had observed and his inability to explain the phenomenon neurologically. I used the exercise to illustrate the profound impact of our thoughts on our physical state. If the stress induced by telling a lie can weaken one's arm, how much more damage could the chronic stress of illness, poverty, poor social relationships, and the global and local effects of wetiko cause to one's health and, potentially, the health of future patients?

CHAPTER 15

From The Lancet to the Light—Reflections on My Journey

Am I mad?

I suspect that if you have read thus far, you may wonder if I am insane, lying, delusional, or maybe—and perhaps rather disturbingly—the real deal.

I can empathise with all these viewpoints since, in the early days, I, too, wondered if what I was experiencing was really happening since it was at odds with my scientific training and conventional beliefs. Only when other people confirmed some of my esoteric observations did I accept that there is so much more to life than materialists would have us believe. Indeed, I have since learned that several of my medical and healthcare worker colleagues have had paranormal experiences that eclipse my own but are reluctant to disclose them for fear of public disdain. I can also empathise with their stance since I have held back from sharing some of my more incredulous events for similar reasons.

At first, I felt very lonely living and working among "normal" people who had never seen the Spirit of a dead person or animal or sensed the love that often comes when the veil is crossed. It was perhaps more challenging for me since I worked within orthodox medicine and was both a clinical and academic doctor with research, teaching, and senior administrative roles within the hospital, and also taught at Swansea

Medical School. Thus, I had to play poacher and game-keeper. I wish I had known then what I know now.

For example, I wish I had known about Dr Yvonne Kason's studies on what she calls Spiritually Transformative Experiences (STEs). This term includes near-death experiences (NDEs), Kundalini/spiritual energy awakenings, psychic experiences, and inspired creativity.

Dr Kason is a retired Canadian family physician and Transpersonal Psychotherapist who had several NDEs both as a child and as an adult. One such NDE, which occurred after a plane crash when she was a young medical doctor, transformed her view of reality and led her to study and counsel STE experiencers. She then co-founded the Spirituality in Healthcare network and wrote six STE-related books. One that I recommend to anyone who has experienced this phenomenon and fears for their sanity is *Touched by Light: Exploring Spiritually Transformative Experiences*, in which she describes the types and characteristics of the various STEs and how to cope with the physical and mental aftermaths.

My hope for this book, which has brought me fully out of my spiritual closet, is that it will act as a metaphysical catalyst to help transform the destructive paradigm in which we live whilst also assisting doctors, other healthcare workers, and anyone who has experienced paranormal phenomena to realise that not only are they not alone, but they are not mad either.

But, then, what is mad?

A Google search of the word "mad" notes that, in the UK, it can mean mentally ill, insane, certifiable, deranged, of unsound mind, etc. Whilst I certainly don't fit the medical criteria for any of the above, like millions of others in this mad, strife-torn world, I often find life, and in particular bereavement, extremely hard to cope with.

After years of coping with my mother's many illnesses and dementia and subsequent death, midwifing a much-loved uncle to his passing as well as the usual mundane but very stressful legal consequences, I was admitted to hospital with Takotsubo cardiomyopathy, broken heart syndrome. Like the young man who developed testicular pain when his perceived soul mate left him, I had somaticised my grief. I learned first-hand how lethal our negative thoughts can be and how easily we can succumb to them. Physically, I slowly recovered but, as mentioned previously, I became so anxious that my doctor prescribed a conventional drug, a selective serotonin reuptake inhibitor (SSRI), which, for me, was poison. I reacted very badly to the medication and had to stop it after three days since my agitation became so severe I really did feel I was going out of my mind. For the majority, these drugs can be life-enhancing, but we all have different metabolisms, and to a few like me, SSRIs can be existentially dangerous.[*]

Fortunately, I quickly learned that one has to have known the depths of despair to truly empathise with and help those who find themselves in that dark pit of despair. In the dark days of our lives, we learn who we really are and how to become more resilient when the subsequent metaphorical tsunami of grief hits the shores of our consciousness. True healing can only come from within our thoughts, with support from friends, communing with nature, particularly trees and birds, exercise, and, for me, the love of a dog, gardening, reflexology, and Indian Head massage therapy.

So, no, like all of us, I am occasionally sad but not clinically mad.

---

[*] If this area of medicine interests you, I can recommend Professor Joanna Moncrieff's eye-opening book, *A Straight Talking Introduction To Psychiatric Drugs: The Truth About How They Work And How to Come Off Them.*" Second edition, 2020. See Recommended Reading for more information.

On the Future of Medicine, Integrated Health, and a Greener Path to Healing

What are my hopes for the future? Firstly, regarding my profession, since my time as a medical student in the 70s, the UK has moved further away from the ancient hands-on apprenticeship model of teaching, which was the norm until the 19th century. Advances in our scientific understanding of the human body, the development of drugs, and a plethora of diagnostic and therapeutic tools made this change both necessary and inevitable. More recently, digital technology has made exponential strides in all aspects of medicine, resulting in changes in medical teaching and clinical practice that were unimaginable 50 years ago.

But in the process of change, we have become increasingly dependent on technology and therapeutic algorithms in a world where one size does not fit all. We have lost much of the essence of "the doctor as a healer." Time constraints, inadequate training, the need to adhere strictly to guidelines, fear of litigation, etc., have severely impacted the doctor-patient interaction, rendering them brief and lacking in eye contact and energetic empathy.

The patient is becoming regarded as a complex machine with defects in certain bits that are not always considered part of the whole body, mind, and Spirit interacting with their environment. Particularly regarding mental health, patients may be given quick-fix drugs simply because the doctor has no time to delve deeper into the actual cause of the problem. As a result, symptoms may merely be suppressed, and the patient dulled into a pseudo-reality.

In the UK, the overall rise in population with a greater proportion of chronically ill elderly patients, plus the enormous cost of diagnostic tests such as magnetic resonance imaging (MRI), positron emission tomography (PET), and lack of health care personnel has almost led to the collapse of our health service and staff have become demoralised.

We desperately need a new healthcare model based on keeping the patient well rather than merely treating them when a disease has become manifest. Orthodox medicine should be more open-minded about what complementary and alternative medicine can offer and consider integrating the two modalities in an Integrated Health (IH) model. To this end, in October 2009, when I was a member of the Royal College of Physicians' now-disbanded Integrated Health Committee, I proposed a definition of IH as follows:

"Integrated health involves assessing an individual's health and well-being as it may be affected by environmental issues at global, regional and local levels, employment status/job satisfaction, interpersonal relationships and coping mechanisms, socio-economic status, ethnic, cultural and religious/spiritual issues and personal habits in terms of risk-taking behaviour (smoking, poor diet, lack of exercise, etc.). Following this assessment and conventional history-taking and examination/investigations, integrated health management involves selecting the best therapeutic tool(s) chosen, where appropriate, from both traditional and complementary/alternative treatment options."

Sadly, the meeting at which I proposed this favoured model was the very last meeting of the Committee. Shortly afterwards, the group was abruptly dissolved, and the Committee could not pursue the concept further.

But there is hope. Recently, at least two major UK projects have been launched that emphasise a "keep-well" rather than "treat-when-ill" approach to medical care.

The first was the 2010 founding of the College of Medicine and Integrated Health (CoM), which arose from the ashes of The Prince's Foundation for Integrated Health—run by the then Prince, now King Charles—and which was closed down around the same time as the Royal College of Physicians' Integrated Health Committee was disbanded. The College of Medicine is chaired by the eminent general practitioner Dr Michael Dixon, who has pioneered social prescribing in his Devon practice and is the current Head of the Royal Medical Household. I share many of his views concerning how we should practice medicine.

In its ten-year manifesto, "Hope for the Future," the College embraces much of what I had tried to encapsulate in my definition of integrated health, submitted to the Royal College of Physicians Integrated Health Committee a year earlier. The College of Medicine's website (*collegeofmedicine.org.uk*) is a treasure chest of information on how best to provide health care. Its manifesto, which includes chapters on Health Inequalities: Creating a Fairer Society; Health and the Environment: Reconnecting with Nature; Social Prescribing: Making Radical Change; Integrated Healthcare: How Complementary and Conventional Medicine Can Work Together; Healthy Food For Everyone, and Medical Training For 21st-Century Healthcare Needs, plus many more topics, is well worth reading.

The second project was the launch of Green Health Wales.[*] A network for sustainable health care in Wales that aims to protect both

---

[*] www.greenhealthwales.co.uk

the people and the planet, Green Health Wales is a relatively new organization that links a myriad groups, including "an international academic collaboration, which annually takes stock of the evolving health impacts of climate change, and the health opportunities that climate action can deliver."

I want to emphasise that, despite disliking how medicine is currently overly reliant on drugs and often lacks compassion, I am not knocking all aspects of conventional practice. If I break a leg, I want an orthopaedic surgeon. If I catch gonorrhoea or chlamydia, apart from declaring it a paranormal event, I would want antibiotics. But the majority of human afflictions have emotional costs; who, for example, could be told they have a life-threatening condition without being mentally traumatised? Stress itself is very much a risk factor for physical illness (heart disease, diabetes, headaches, gastrointestinal disorders, recurrent Herpes simplex infections, etc.) and mental disorders such as anxiety and depression. Here is where I feel Complementary and Alternative Medicine practitioners may prove invaluable.

On the Future of Humanity, Religion, and Life's Purpose

I hope that, globally, we will become less focused on our tribal religious dogma and more open to each of us having a direct link to Spirit without intermediaries. So many of the world's greatest religions have a very dark side that often involves hatred of anyone who does not share the same belief system. Religious elders may abuse their power, which can result in holy wars, stigmatisation of minority groups, and appalling abuse of women and children. If there is to be world peace, we must reject extreme religious dogma and adopt a more spiritual and eclectic approach to how we live our lives.

In her book *Infinite Mind: Science of the Human Vibrations of Consciousness*, published in 1995, Dr Valerie Hunt quoted Buddha's wisdom, which encapsulates what I believe:

- "Do not believe what you have heard.
- Do not believe in tradition, because it is handed down many generations.
- Do not believe in anything that has been spoken of many times.
- Do not believe because the written statements come from some old sage.
- Do not believe in conjecture.
- Do not believe in authority or teachers or elders.
- But after careful observation and analysis, when it agrees with reason, and it will benefit one and all, then accept it and live by it."

For healthcare workers involved in making diagnoses, I would expand this to include:

- Trust your gut, and if you don't sense that conventional diagnostic algorithms are correct, then check again and maybe even order more investigations until your gut, heart, and brain are in harmony.

But if we abandon religious dogma, what can fill the void? And are there simple guidelines we can follow? I believe there are. As a child, I was fascinated by Albert Einstein and his quotations. I particularly cherished "Only a life lived for others is a life worthwhile." It seems a noble way to approach one's journey on Earth.

While researching this book, I came across a paper by Tal Gur about Einstein's quotation. A lifestyle entrepreneur, nomad capitalist, and author of several books, including *The Art of Fully Living— 1 Man, 10 Years, 100 Life Goals*, Gur founded Elevate Society to help people "make a bigger, more conscious impact on society," and in his insightful paper, he discusses eleven ways Einstein's edict can be manifested.* These comprise: Humanitarian work, Healthcare and Medicine, Social work and Counselling, Education and Teaching, Community Service, Philanthropy, Mentoring and Coaching, Advocacy and Activism, Parenting and Family, Random Acts of Kindness, and Being an Inspirational Role Model.

Gur's conclusion that "Only a life lived for others is a life worthwhile" underscores the idea that a life centred on service, empathy, and making a positive impact on the lives of others is truly meaningful and fulfilling. It highlights the diverse ways in which individuals can

---

* https://elevatesociety.com/only-a-life-lived-for/

contribute to the betterment of society and inspires others to do the same.

I started this book by mentioning the short story I wrote in 2007 on "any aspect of medical science or health—past, present, or future" for a competition run by The Lancet medical journal for their December edition. Some of what I wrote in that story was true; the rest came straight from my imagination. Curiously, some of what I imagined, including predicting the occurrence of a pandemic and associated changes in medical practice, came true. How can we explain that? And how can we explain all the other anomalous experiences I, and countless people worldwide, have also had? We can't. Granted, some of them can be explained by coincidences and/or the imagination of an informed mind. However, throughout my life and career, I have witnessed many paranormal occurrences and heard many strange and inexplicable stories that fit the category of "anomalous experiences." I would have liked to share more of them here, but due to space constraints, I must leave those for a later book.

For now, I shall end this book by sharing a story that resonates with me on many levels. Not the least of which is that it is a superb example of a left-brained, highly-credentialed, and distinguished professional who dared to challenge the establishment's view of reality and face the fear of being called mad.

Dr Elizabeth Lloyd Mayer was a respected American psychoanalyst, researcher and teacher when, in 1991, her daughter's rare and precious harp was stolen from a performance venue. Despite Mayer's best efforts involving the police, musical instrument dealers, newsletters to the American Harp Society, and a TV news story, the harp remained lost. In desperation, Mayer reluctantly asked a dowser named Harold McCoy, who lived some 2000 miles away, if he could help. Within two days, Harold located the house where the harp had been taken, and eventually, the harp was returned. Mayer was dumbfounded; her life-long view of reality had been turned upside down.

In her book *Extraordinary Knowing: Science, Skepticism, and the Inexplicable Powers of the Human Mind*, Mayer recalls many sleepless nights trying to rationalise what had happened within her Western orthodox training and mindset. She recounts how she was forced into re-evaluating her beliefs and subsequently changed the entire direction of her research to understand such anomalous events and how, when her new interest became known, many people, including her colleagues and patients, started privately sharing their own experiences.

One such example was an eminent brain surgeon who had a phenomenal success rate, who consulted Mayer in a last resort attempt to find and heal the source of years of intractable headaches, which, on examination, seemed to have no physical cause. The surgeon confided that he used to sit by his patients' bedsides until a bright light appeared above their heads, which he "knew" was a sign that it was safe to operate. But knowing that he couldn't possibly risk revealing that to his students, he gave up teaching. On probing further, Mayer discovered that the surgeon's crippling headaches started the very same day he gave up teaching!

Like Elizabeth Mayer, I, too, found that the more I talked about my paranormal occurrences, the more sometimes even senior colleagues confided their experiences to me. Sadly, I cannot write about some of the most amazing stories as the individuals involved are still afraid of being labelled psychotic or delusional.

But I am most definitely *not* mad. And neither are the thousands of people worldwide and throughout history who have dared to share their "paranormal" experiences.

If you are among them, I sincerely hope that this book will alleviate your fears of being thought crazy and open sceptical minds to the need for us all to start viewing life through a less materialistic lens and become more aware that we are all connected and are essentially energetic consciousness temporarily enclosed in human flesh.

Epilogue

This book has had a very long gestation; it was perhaps conceived when I first met the Spirit girl I played with in childhood and wondered why no one else could see her. Or maybe it was when I watched in awe and curiosity as my carefully nurtured frogspawn transformed into tadpoles and tiny froglets. The curiosity and tenacity I had as a child moulded me into a dogged and internationally recognised researcher, so when I experienced a re-emergence of anomalous childhood encounters it was inevitable that I would seek explanations.

Whilst I still struggle to comprehend much of what I've observed and why my "gift" suddenly disappeared when my challenging elderly mother moved in with me, I have developed a more profound acceptance of paranormal experiences. As a result, I have counselled and reassured many often fearful people who privately shared their strange experiences. I am planning a second book that will include some of my more esoteric encounters and new stories from other, mainly professional friends and colleagues.

Finally, whilst researching this book, I came across an old school notebook in which, as a young teenager living in a grim cold tin shed, I had written that when I was grown up, I would write an autobiography in which the later chapters would be about faith healing! If I had come from a particularly spiritual and/or literary background, this teenage prediction would not seem strange. But given that Dad was a disabled bus driver and Mum worked on her market stall with little money for books or even holidays, such aspirations were, to say the least, fanciful. I had forgotten entirely this teenage prediction, but I believe we all have a sacred pre-life contract to fulfil when we are born.

I know that mine included writing this book.

Anona Blackwell, Summer 2024

APPENDIX I

Reflections on Medical Advances 2007-2107

A predictive essay (some of which came true) written in 2007 for a Lancet competition but never submitted.

A woman shuffled into the consulting room, and the spirit of a child scampered after her, seemingly anxious not to be too far away from mum, as if attached by an ethereal rubber band. The child's energy faded as the doctor focused on the mother's problem to create the sacred space of healing. The patient had intractable pelvic pain which had been extensively but fruitlessly investigated for years. Repeat screening for infection was a last forlorn attempt to find a cure. The doctor asked about her patient's gynaecological and obstetric history. The woman said that she'd had a daughter who had died five years previously in an accident, shortly before the pain had started. She added, 'Actually doctor I've just been to see a medium before coming here and apparently my little girl follows me everywhere… You know part of my soul left when my little girl died'.

The doctor understood but could only try to share the woman's grief and dare not tell that she, too, had seen the child. She held the woman's hand and sent compassion to her and the little lost soul who followed her mum everywhere, even into a hospital clinic. Years of bereavement counselling, antidepressants, and painkillers had not helped the emotional pain, which seemed to stay locked deep within the tissues of the woman's body. The doctor intuitively sensed the problem but could not help since it was 2007, and orthodox medical minds were still closed to the concept that unresolved emotions were an energy form which could produce physical pain. When no infection was found the woman left. The doctor felt inadequate at her inability to heal the souls of this mother and her child. All she could do was pray that the woman's grief did not eventually find solace in a physical disease.

The clinic was over, and the doctor had a challenging lunchtime meeting to attend. A cloud of stress, sickness, anger, fear and despair trailed her colleagues as they entered the room, reflecting what they had been exposed to all morning. Sensing the emotions, the doctor felt sick.

In 2005, the work of the Institute of Noetic Science's chief scientist, Dean Radin and social scientist Marilyn Schlitz, cited in Lynne McTaggart's book *The Intention Experiment*,* suggested that others can indeed register our gut emotions. The doctor wished everyone understood that healing and negative emotions don't mix, but this was still not widely known. At the end of the meeting, she was glad to escape to the relative sanctuary of her office.

It was the darkest days of healing when doctors were morphed from healers into medical technicians who increasingly knew more and more about less and less, curing many but healing few. They were better paid but had a sadness of the soul they could not articulate. Their power to heal was drained by a culture in which numbers seen per pound were the driving force, and time was of the essence. It was tick-box medicine when many knew a lot about a little and even less about the wisdom needed to solve many of their patient's problems.

Over a hundred years on and how we deride the way we perceived illness in those days! In 2007, the belief that consciousness is an energy that transcends space and time was widely considered to be the musings of the mad and sad. Those few who preferred to live in the seemingly

APPENDIX I

schizophrenic world of quantum physics where objects could be in two places simultaneously, the only time was in the now, and matter was ultimately incarnate light were a small but increasingly vocal group.

We now know that truly whole people are not just the sum of their parts. But the medical paradigm dictated by Newtonian physics ruled back then. Pharmaceutical companies produced a plethora of chemical cures for illnesses, many of which did not actually begin in the physical body but manifested there. In the latter part of the 20th century, menopause was considered an "illness" that needed treatment rather than being accepted as part of the natural cycle of life. This spawned a vast array of widely used hormone replacement therapies. Obesity was endemic, yet few approaches to its control seemed able to effect sustained health, and anxiety and depression were rife. The standard of living had never been higher, but doctors' waiting rooms overflowed with patients. The psycho-neuroimmunological effects of the physical and energetic environments in which people lived caused many illnesses, but little could reduce those. The roles of hospital staff were constantly being re-defined, and uncertainty and fear were rife, resulting in stress and high rates of sickness. It seemed an endless cycle. Training for young doctors was also constantly changing, and no one knew what the future might hold. Hospitals were not an ideal healing place for patients, staff or trainees. But all was to change in 2012 when a quantum shift in global consciousness finally forced a 180-degree turn in the practice of Western Medicine.

No one knows when the shift started, but towards the end of the 20th century, the science of human consciousness was under study in a few laboratories. Professor Gary Schwartz, best known for his pioneering work on cellular memory, led one of the most eminent at the University of Arizona. It seems laughable now, but in 2007, the consensus was that memory was somehow stored in the brain rather than diffusely in the body's energy field and beyond. Schwartz's early work, showing that heat-shocked bacteria survived better when healers held their hands near the culture pots, was less well-known. But this only worked when the healers themselves were well at all levels. Curiously, the bacteria also survived better if the healer primed their healing power by first giving healing to a person, suggesting that good intent, perhaps reflected in a good bedside manner, was also important.

While most people understood at gut level that what differentiated a good physician from a great one was a good bedside manner, the full impact of Schwartz's findings was not appreciated until years later when further experiments showed that many outcomes, from response to drugs and even surgical procedures, were better when health workers cleared their energy fields before going to work. Later studies revealed that health workers with good bedside manners also had more love, compassion, and less fear and unresolved rage than colleagues with poorer clinical outcomes.

It seems so obvious now that a relaxed and focused team will produce better results than one where one or more members have attitude problems that may create a negative energy field which can affect other team members and ultimately adversely affect patient care.

Schwartz's team also used devices to measure the energy emanating from a group of healers' hands. They found that even just holding their hands near a sealed box containing cut geranium leaves resulted in a positive increase in biophoton release. But interesting though it was, since this data did not sit well within a Newtonian mindset, Schwartz's work remained largely unknown within the UK medical fraternity. However, Schwartz did have an ally whose influence helped increase general awareness of his work—an investigative journalist named Lynne

McTaggart, who was fascinated by everything relating to what she termed "The Field." Her book of the same name has remained a classic for over 100 years since its publication in 2001.‡ Back then, the mainstream had yet to embrace the concept of a reality in which we all live within a universal energy field where everything is interconnected in space and time. McTaggart's books and many workshops were instrumental in bringing these ideas to the general population. Energy healing, dowsing, mediumship, and, in particular, the power of prayer, are among many topics that seem to find an explanation when viewed from a Quantum rather than Newtonian paradigm.

In 2007, McTaggart collaborated with Schwartz's team on The Intention Experiment, which involved thousands of people praying for a geranium leaf to produce more photons than an unprayed for control leaf in Schwartz's laboratory. This led to further studies over the years, eventually showing that thoughts can influence matter—a scary concept in the early 21st century since thoughts can be positive or negative. When this became known, people became much more aware of how their thoughts affected their health and added to the increasingly toxic world created by negative emotions entering The Field.

In the meantime, while Schwartz was doing his work in Arizona, another scientist, Professor Konstantin Korotkov, from St Petersburg in Russia, was developing a device to measure and evaluate the aura or human energy field. The technique, which was a development of Kirlian photography, was known as Gas Discharge Visualisation (GDV). The computerised images that Korotkov's device produced were called beograms.

Korotkov had shown that, when meditating, an individual's beogram dramatically changed. Korotkov had also experimented with Ayahuasca, the mind-altering hallucinogen made from so-called teacher plants that

Amazonian shamans use to enter altered states of reality. Korotkov found that when he drank the potion, his beogram suggested that his left brain was no longer functioning normally. Within native shamanic beliefs, a person can gain greater insight and knowledge from taking teacher plant medicines. Korotkov's work also suggested that the beograms of naturally gifted mediums differed, with part of the aura around their heads vibrating at levels his machine could not measure. GDV was not widely available in the UK in the first decade of the 21st century. Because it was relatively insensitive, it initially had limited use in medicine.

The following section was imaginative fiction, although some of it did actually happen.

However, following a sudden breakthrough in 2010 with the invention of quantum computers that could work at room temperature, the world of GDV interpretation took a quantum leap in sensitivity and specificity, eventually leading to the development of computerised home diagnostics (CHD), which have become so much a part of our culture.[†]

It would have been inconceivable in 2007 that routine medical checks would one day be done whilst sitting at a home computer using a very advanced form of the original Korotkov GDV device. Korotkov conceived that one could identify diseases simply by holding one's hand on a metal disc, passing a small electric current through it, and then recording the energy that bounced back to the camera. However, the advent of quantum computers made the device capable of accurate diagnoses.

Cheap superconductors that worked at room temperature were invented in the 2020s. Shortly after, a bright young quantum physicist came across an old research paper in which the idea of using superconductors with GDV filters had been mooted. The physicist's subsequent research eventually led to even more sensitive GDV devices that incorporated many superconducting crystal discs. These permitted the production of the filtered electromagnetic equivalent of ultrasound, which bounced energy off selected molecules and cellular components. The reflected electromagnetic energy "read" the patients' health more accurately than any other combination of tests previously devised.

By 2023, GDV technology was so advanced that it could detect illness in a person's energy field before it manifested in their physical body. The local hospital's virtual reality (VR) suite, where patients also received cognitive behaviour therapy appropriate to their energy field defect, then conducted any necessary adjustments. These units were staffed by nurse practitioners who did 30 minutes of compulsory meditation before being allowed to enter. Anyone whose energy field was still not in healing mode was sent home for rest or underwent a mandatory energy field adjustment before being allowed near their patients. Non-clinical staff were never allowed into healing areas because the energy of anger and frustration they sometimes brought with them, which the GDV devices detected, affected the energetic infrastructure of the healing suites. GDV screening of all health staff became mandatory in 2025. In 2030, a national scandal arose when a two-million-pound healing suite was rendered useless by the negative energy of an irate chief executive who forced himself into a VR healing unit to speak to his estranged wife. After that, entering such units without verified energy clearance became a sackable offence.

Looking back, it seems strange to us now, but in 2007, it was common for non-clinical offices to be located within healing units with direct access to patients and staff. Negative energy, which we now know to be highly harmful, was not measurable then and hence was often overlooked. However, as our understanding of energy fields and their impact on health grew, so did our healthcare practices. We began to realise the importance of maintaining a positive energy environment for healing, leading to developing and implementing GDV technology in healthcare.

By 2020, computerised home diagnostics carried out much of the basic diagnostic work formerly done by general practitioners. After patients had logged on for their six-monthly GDV health screens, dietary and lifestyle advice was given online. If any serious complaint was noted, online appointments in the relevant specialist units were made. A side benefit of technological advances was that GDV devices could also pick up good and bad energy in food and other products. Immediate readouts of toxins, vitamins and life force energy became possible, which had a profound effect on people's dietary choices and smoking habits. By 2040, no one smoked tobacco and two-thirds of the population had become exclusively vegetarian. Organic, "animal-friendly" meat production was the norm for the rest. The change to a largely vegetarian economy dramatically affected the global economy and, fortuitously, global warming. The net effect was that people lived longer and were much healthier. By 2050, the average retirement age was 72.

Globally, the most profound effect on international well-being occurred directly from research on human consciousness, which, in 2031, conclusively showed that death is "just" a change of the vibrational frequency of human consciousness and that death of consciousness never occurs. In 2035, further work showed that the so-called akashic records of all living beings' activities exist at an energetic level in non-ordinary reality. This awakened people to how devastating negative thoughts could be for them and others, which led to a not-so-altruistic 180-degree change in how they lived. The concept of universal interconnectedness gained widespread acceptance, significantly decreasing infant mortality and birth rates as emotional and physical well-being became globally accessible.

Severe physical, emotional and spiritual illnesses became rare. When illness beyond the remit of energy nurse practitioners occurred, three main groups of doctors treated it: surgeons, specialist physicians, and doctor shamans.

Surgeons worked on the lowest vibrational diseases when they manifested as physical tumours, degenerative diseases, or traumatic events. Physicians cured illness when it displayed at the molecular level, whilst the most gifted doctors—the doctor shamans—worked on the vibration of consciousness and spirit. These doctors had 30 years of training before being allowed to practice unsupervised and were skilled in general medicine, psychoneuroimmunology, and spiritual philosophy. They were also apprenticed to the modern equivalent of a shaman who entered altered states of consciousness to access other realms of reality and bring back the knowledge required to help each patient. Doctor shamans never married and reproduced only by cloning with no parental duties to defocus their healing powers. They enjoyed great privileges but also endured great personal sacrifice and were intuitively called to this role from childhood, with training starting from age eight in most regions. These are the healers to whom the woman whose Spirit child still followed her in 2007 would have been referred if they had existed. They would have helped the child go fully into the vibration of light and helped the mother retrieve the lost parts of her soul.

That was the relatively idyllic state of medicine till 2101, when the second avian influenza pandemic occurred, seeded by several mini tsunamis hitting the southern hemisphere, which had seen sporadic avian flu outbreaks in wild birds. Unfortunately, the pandemic spread as thousands of international volunteers sent to help the surviving populations returned to their respective countries. This drove further global economic and cultural change, which, once again, was dramatically mirrored in the practice of medicine.

But that's another story.

---

* Cited by Lynne McTaggart in *The Intention Experiment*, 2007

‡ McTaggart L, *The Field* 2001

† In his book *Energy of Consciousness*, published in 2014, which I read in April 2022, Korotkov says, "I believe that in some time, systems of (home) monitoring and long-term control of health state on computer basis will start being actively developed in the world." He goes on to describe a possible management plan very similar to what I had predicted would result from his work seven years previously! In my opinion, Korotkov is a genius, and *Energy of Consciousness* is a treasure trove of knowledge and hope for the future.

APPENDIX II

HRT is for Women Who go Mad at the Menopause

*Lancet Dissecting Room Jabs & Jibes,
volume 357, issue 9268, p1632, May 19, 2001
Copyright Elsevier with permission.*

As a student I asked a consultant gynaecologist, "What's HRT?" He replied, "Its Hormone Replacement Therapy, we use it for women who go mad at the menopause." During the 1970s in the UK, HRT was viewed with suspicion. Our undergraduate textbook only briefly mentioned hot flushes and (over)emphasised the benefits of the menopause: "for many women the menopause is a blessed relief from the burden of childbearing."

Over the ensuing years I learnt much about HRT, but nothing prepared me for the physiological onslaught that can hit you when your oestrogen finally runs out. Being fat, I had hoped that I would have few menopausal symptoms and, apart from buying a fan and not bulk buying tampons, I decided to wait and see.

Unfortunately menopausal symptoms creep up on you—how do you know what a hot flush is when you've never had one before. At night you learn to "sleep" with one leg outside the duvet, you become giddy in the mornings at first and then for most of the day, compensate by holding onto the examination couch in clinics and to the lectern when lecturing. My lethargy increased, so I bought a carbon monoxide monitor and installed a new boiler to exclude some hidden toxin. I still managed to work, but speaking at international meetings needed Herculean effort. Finally one December night, after suffering many hot flushes by proxy, my Jack Russell/sleeping partner (JR), became uncharacteristically ratty. With a frustrated "woof" that's normally reserved for cats he sees but cannot reach, JR voted with his paws, jumped off the bed and lay on the floor, head buried desolately in his paws! To compound matters I found I had hypertension and, after a 30lb-weight loss, my menses stopped abruptly and intermittent attacks of intense calmness and surreal separation of mind and spirit ensued. I finally decided to seek help when, during one such episode, I was in the middle of a clinic.

A kind (male) consultant physician was summoned who, having found no cause for my plethora of symptoms, gently asked if I could be pregnant or depressed. My female colleagues were highly amused and commented that it was a new millennium and there had recently been a new, albeit, manmade "star" in the sky—perhaps I had been impregnated with a new messianic variant JC virus, I thought. My male colleagues, God bless them, did not think pregnancy was implausible but whatever was wrong, I felt increasingly wretched and wondered if I really was (just) depressed.

I became one of those patients who resort to writing symptoms on scraps of paper and searching the internet for explanations—it is surprising what you find under oestradiol and neurotransmitters. It was time to see my GP for HRT—you know the drug you give to women who go mad at the menopause. After 6 days of HRT, JR was back to nocturnal snuggle duties and by 6 weeks I felt upgraded from 8 to 256 megabytes of RAM (more realistically 128 perhaps) with a new processor to boot!

Appendix II

Learning Points
1. Stick your patches on before you shower or they fall off.
2. If you are a middle-aged, dog-tired woman whose partner/JR will not snuggle any more, and you find that your name badge has become an essential aide memoire, then think about taking HRT. It will almost certainly be more cost-effective than changing your boiler/partner and will keep the dog happy!

Anona Blackwell Published: May 19, 2001

APPENDIX III

Anam Cara*

You are the dew on the morning rose
You are the smell of sun-dried clothes
You are the seagull soaring on high,
You are the sunset in an Autumn sky.
You are the otter tumbling in glee,
You are the joy of my dog on my knee.
You are a hot shower after a drenching with rain,
You are the one who always eases my pain.
You are the bluebells in an oak wood,
You are the essence of all that is good.
You are a warm fire on a cold winter's night,
You are a candle in a room with no light.
You are the dolphin whose spirit is free,
You are my friend and so special to me

---

* Gaelic word meaning Soul friend... one who advises the right spiritual path with unconditional love.

Recommended Reading

Some of My Favourite Authors and Their Books

MARK ANTHONY—*The Afterlife Frequency. The Scientific Proof of Spiritual Contact and How That Awareness Will Change Your Life* (2021)

Mark Anthony, also known as the Psychic Lawyer, introduces his concept of the electromagnetic soul in this book. He covers phenomena such as Near-Death Experiences, Death Bed Visions, Mediumship, and more. I suggest checking out his YouTube material since his depth of knowledge and gentle sense of humour make for an informative and enjoyable experience. https://afterlifefrequency.com

PMH ATWATER—*The Big Book of Near-Death Experiences. The Ultimate Guide to the NDE and its After effects* (2007)

This encyclopaedic book of over 470 pages does precisely what it says on the tin. Atwater states in the introduction that it takes a "360-degree look at the entire near-death phenomenon in all its positive and negative aspects." Whilst its approach is academic, appropriate graphics and even the odd cartoon help make it easy to grasp. It also includes a helpful eight-page glossary of new words. This is another must-read for all those seeking a deeper understanding of the concepts. https://www.pmhatwater.com

EVELYN ELSAESSER—*Spontaneous Contacts with the Deceased—A large-scale international survey reveals the circumstances, lived experiences and beneficial impact of After Death Communications (ADCs)* (2023)
This book is surprisingly readable despite being based on an academic research project that I outlined in chapter 12. Elsaesser includes many fascinating and thought-provoking descriptions of ADCs, making the book a page-turner for both academics and those who just have an interest in this area. https://www.evelynelsaesser.com

VALERIE V HUNT—*Infinite Mind: Science of the Human Vibrations of Consciousness* (1989)
Despite being published some 34 years ago, *Infinite Mind* remains a treasure trove of the science of the human energy field. It describes what Hunt calls the new electromagnetic model of illness and health. Professor Hunt notes that people who have had mystical experiences may feel they are losing their minds, and some even asked her if they were sane. She writes: "I always answer, 'if you can co-experience mystical and material reality—if you know the difference, yet can integrate and use the force of this awareness—then you are not merely sane but super sane.'" When I first read it in 2006, its timeless wisdom comforted me.

YVONNE KASON—*Touched by The Light: Exploring Spiritually Transformative Experiences* (2019)
This book is a must-read for anyone who has had a spiritual awakening/transformation since some consequences, such as suddenly sensing dead people, can be alarming. Kason describes all aspects of a Kundalini awakening and how to cope with the distressing psychic symptoms that may occur. https://dryvonnekason.com

KONSTANTIN KOROTKOV—*The Energy of Consciousness* (2014)
Konstantin Korotkov, PhD is a professor of Computer Science and Biophysics at Saint Petersburg Federal University of Informational Technologies, Mechanics and Optics, President of the International Union for Medical and Applied Bioelectrography, and a Member of the Editorial Board: Journal of Alternative and Complementary Medicine and Journal of Science of Healing Outcomes. He's also authored many books. My favourite is *The Energy of Consciousness*, in which Korotkov describes his studies using an electrophotonic imaging technique called Gas discharge Visualisation (GDV) based on Kirlian photography, which assesses the human energy field in health and disease.

Korotkov developed the Kirlians' invention into what he calls the Bio-Well GDV camera and used modern computer software to analyse his patients' electromagnetic fields or auras, which, apparently, correlate with sympathetic and parasympathetic activity. His GDV device also shows the ostensive location and size of human chakras, the energy centres in the body which are linked to specific nerve bundles and internal organs and can seemingly energetically pick up possible health issues before they have manifested clinically.

From my verified "paranormal" sensing of my Jack Russell's testicular cancer months before it became a physical tumour, the childhood memory of my late father's odd vibrations when he had a heart attack, and many anomalous events throughout my long medical career, I know that ill health affects the energy body in which our physical form exists and this can be detected. My (albeit limited) experiences concur with Korotkov's findings.

In the book, Korotkov shares his belief that "in some time, systems of monitoring and long-term control of health state on computer basis will start being actively developed in the world." Korotkov suggests that in future it may be feasible to use a device at home that will take a set of parameters and send the results to an internet database for analysis. If anything abnormal is found, appropriate intervention would be taken.

This is one of my all-time-favourite books, which links science with spirituality. It is well-written, humorous, and easy to understand despite some of the complex ideas Korotkov covers. It also has intriguing chapter titles like *What is Consciousness?* and *Can Love Be Measured?* In the latter, he concludes, "So it turns out that Love is really the only force that can withstand Evil and save Humanity from the coming catastrophes." Let's hope he is right.

BRUCE LIPTON—*The Biology of Belief: Unleashing the Power of Consciousness, Matter, and Miracles* (2005).
Dr Lipton is a cell biologist, teacher, writer, and a pioneer in the field of epigenetics. Having completed my first biology/biophysics degree at Kings College London, whose biophysics department was deeply involved in the discovery of DNA structure in 1953, I was imbued with the supremacy of our genome. However, we now know that environmental factors, behaviour, thoughts, and beliefs can epigenetically affect gene expression. *The Biology of Belief* provides a guide to epigenetics and includes sections on the placebo and nocebo effects. Dr Lipton's book makes a complex subject easy to understand. https://www.brucelipton.com

ELIZABETH LLOYD MAYER—*Extraordinary Knowing: Science, Skepticism, And The Inexplicable Powers Of The Human Mind* (2007).
This book was published two years after Dr Mayer's tragic death from complications of a dreadful disease, scleroderma, at the age of 56. In her only YouTube presentation she gives a brief outline of how a left-brained

psychoanalyst, researcher, and clinician became obsessed with anomalous occurrences after a dowser who lived some 2000 miles away was able to locate her daughter's lost harp. Her vitality, intellect, passion, and sense of humour are so evident in her video that one wonders how much humanity has lost with her untimely death. Mayer's book is a mother lode of paranormal experiences, research, and many stories obtained during her quest to explain the discovery of the lost harp. It's an easy read and parallels, in part for me, my attempts to resolve the conflict between my scientific training and my personal direct experience of the paranormal. https://www.youtube.com/watch?v=AClVSWvNsWw

LYNNE McTAGGART—*The Field: The Quest For The Secret Force Of The Universe* (2003) and *The Intention Experiment* (2007).
Lynne McTaggart has written seven books in total. But my favourite is *The Field*, not the least because reading it in 2003 saved my sanity by providing a scientific basis for many of the paranormal events I was experiencing. In her chapter on "The Healing Field," McTaggart says that illness may be caused by isolation and lack of connection with the collective health of the Field and the community. She adds that the most essential treatment doctors can give is to hope for the health and well-being of their patients… wise words indeed. *The Intention Experiment* is another favourite. It offers a deep exploration of the many fascinating aspects of the power of intention/prayer. Both books are highly informative, and McTaggart's website (lynnemctaggart.com), with links to many of her free broadcasts and details of teaching events, is worth exploring. https://lynnemctaggart.com

JOANNA MONCRIEFF—*A Straight-Talking Introduction to Psychiatric Drugs: The Truth About How They Work And How to Come Off Them* (2nd edition 2020)
I acquired Moncrieff's book to get a better understanding of psychoactive drugs after I had a scary reaction to a selective serotonin reuptake inhibitor. She describes how many of our typical responses to life's adversities have become medicalised by the pharmaceutical industry, doctors, and even patients seeking rapid solace from their woes. Professor Moncrief discusses a wide range of psychoactive drugs, their history, indications, side effects, etc. It's a helpful book for those who may require such drugs so they can make fully informed decisions. https://joannamoncrieff.com

RAYMOND MOODY—*Life After Life: Actual Case Histories That Reveal There is Life After Death* (1975)
Life After Life is Dr Moody's classic book in which he first introduced the term near-Death Experiences (NDEs). Though written almost 50 years ago, it remains relevant to anyone who wishes to learn the basic features of NDEs and the history of this phenomenon.

RAYMOND MOODY AND PAUL PERRY—*Proof of Life After Life: 7 reasons to Believe There is an Afterlife* (2023)
Dr Moody's latest book, co-authored with Paul Perry, is essential for anyone interested in NDEs. Among many topics, it covers shared death and out-of-body experiences, precognition, and terminal lucidity. The authors have included reports of numerous paranormal experiences and how these have affected the individuals involved. It is well-written, easy to understand, and makes for relaxing bedtime reading. https://www.lifeafterlife.com

RECOMMENDED READING

CAROLINE MYSS—*Sacred Contracts: Awakening Your Divine Potential* (2001). Caroline Myss is an American teacher, writer, medical intuitive, and mystic. I have attended many of her workshops and love her no-nonsense but often humorous teaching style.

I first read *Sacred Contracts* in 2003 at the beginning of my spiritual re-awakening. I must admit I did not understand or even know about Jung's concept of the collective unconscious, archetypal patterns or even the basics of the chakra system, which are all covered in this book. As a result, I initially found it hard-going. But, guided by her brilliant insights, it helped lead me into the magical world of human consciousness. Myss expands Jung's basic archetypes into dozens of easily recognisable exemplars, describing their "light" and "shadow" attributes. It enables you to recognise behaviour patterns in yourself and others. I found it invaluable when making a holistic assessment of my patients and only wish *Sacred Contracts* were part of medical training, as it should be.

You can find details of Myss's many other books (*Anatomy of the Spirit* and *Invisible Acts of Power* are my other favourites), events, workshops, and lots of free resources about archetypes, the chakra system, sacred contracts, and many videos on her website. It's also worth checking out her material on YouTube. https://www.myss.com.

RUPERT SHELDRAKE is a biologist, and prolific researcher, teacher, and writer. He has written nine books and co-authored six more, including *A New Science of Life: The Hypothesis of Morphic Resonance* (1999), *Dogs That Know When Their Owners Are Coming Home: And Other Unexplained Powers of Animals* (1999), *Chaos Creativity and Cosmic Consciousness* (2001), and *The Science Delusion: Freeing the spirit of Enquiry* (2012). A scientific free-thinker who, like Bruce Lipton, challenges scientific dogma, Sheldrake is best known for researching how dogs know when their owners are coming home and the intellectually fascinating subject of morphic resonance and morphic fields.

As a child, I loved to climb trees and always scraped my knees. I thought it was magical that my body knew how to repair itself. However, Sheldrake's morphic field hypothesis would suggest that we have an individual default energetic morphic template our body uses to repair itself. Similarly, I used to be in awe of the complexity of robins' and wrens' nests and could not understand how tiny birds knew what to do. Again, Sheldrake's idea is that individual species receive information by energetically linking up with the vibration of the universal consciousness that resonates most closely with their own. As I understand it, each species is born with its own energetic/morphic field linked by morphic resonance to its collective unconscious memory, a species-specific energetic knowledge or blueprint.

I'm convinced that, like Korotkov, Rupert Sheldrake is a genius with ideas that eventually will be proven. Having thus far read only four of his books, I cannot choose a favourite, but I suspect it would be *A New Science of Life*, first published in 1981. Whilst intellectually challenging, it is well worth the effort. Sheldrake's website is a mine of information. https://www.sheldrake.org

CHARLES T. TART—*The End of Materialism: How Evidence of the Paranormal Is Bringing Science and Spirit Together* (2009).
I learned a lot from Professor Tart's book and used his Western Creed (as described in chapter 14) when teaching medical students. This book covers areas of parapsychology similar to those of Mark Anthony in *The Afterlife Frequency* but is more research-based. I found it interesting and easy to read, and it also provides plenty of teaching material. https://closertotruth.com/contributor/charlestart

RECOMMENDED READING

BRIAN WEISS—*Many Lives, Many Masters: The True Story of a Prominent Psychiatrist, His Young Patient and the Past Life Therapy That Changed Both Their Lives* (1988)

Brian Weiss, a Yale University School of Medicine graduate, is a psychiatrist and hypnotherapist who specialises in past and future life regression and survival of the soul. He's written six very readable books on aspects of the above, including, *Through Time into Healing: Discovering the Power of Regression Therapy to Erase Trauma and Transform Mind, Body and Relationships* (1993); *Only Love is Real: A Story of Soulmates Reunited* (1996); *Messages From the Masters: Tapping into the Power of Love* (1999); *Same Soul, Many Bodies: Discover the Healing Power of Future Lives through Progression Therapy* (2004); and *Miracles Happen: The Transformational Healing Power of Past Life Memories* (2011) co-authored with his daughter Amy Weiss.

If the idea of past/future lives interests you, I suggest reading the above books in the order they were published since I found it easier to understand the subject matter. https://www.brianweiss.com

About the Author

DR ANONA BLACKWELL is a retired consultant in Genital-Urinary Medicine who was an internationally recognised expert in genital tract infections for 25 years. She completed her BSc in biology/biophysics at Kings College London and attained a diploma in comparative religions in 1970. She studied medicine at Westminster Medical School and undertook her junior doctor training at the Middlesex and St Thomas' Hospitals in London before commencing her research and eventually becoming a senior registrar and lecturer in Genito-Urinary Medicine at St. Thomas'. Her team's work on anaerobic vaginal infections resulted in two Lancet-published papers in the early 80s, one of which permanently changed UK clinical practice for the treatment of anaerobic/bacterial vaginosis.

Whilst at St. Thomas' Dr. Blackwell also had several paranormal experiences, including sensing the presence of patients' late relatives. However, her most extraordinary anomalous encounters occurred when she moved to a consultant post in Swansea in 1985, where, with local colleagues, she continued her research investigating the aetiology of pelvic infection. This resulted in a third Lancet-published paper in 1993.

In 1996, she was invited to join a small group of eminent international scientists and clinicians at a closed Pelvic Infection workshop at the Royal College of Obstetricians and Gynaecologists in London. Her team's publication was again instrumental in facilitating change in clinical practice.

Dr Blackwell had a busy clinical, teaching and administrative workload and was firmly grounded in orthodox practice. However, a premonition of a colleague's unexpected demise led her to recall paranormal events from her childhood, and she became fascinated with studying human consciousness. She trained as a spiritual healer and attended countless workshops on metaphysics, shamanism, neuro-linguistic programming, crystal healing, Ayurvedic medicine, etc., to gain greater understanding of how medical practice could be improved.

Having been awarded a Fellowship of the Royal College of Physicians (FRCP) for clinical excellence, she was invited to join the RCP's Integrated Health Committee in 2006, where she served until it was dissolved in 2010.

Dr Blackwell's autobiography focuses on her clinical career, numerous paranormal experiences, how she has tried to make sense of her encounters with the Spirit world and even meeting Prince/King Charles. It includes discussions on near-death experiences, pre-life sacred contracts, psychometry, precognition, mediumship and much more. She concludes that orthodox medicine has much to learn from appreciating that the human body is not just a complex machine but is truly consciousness/Spirit in physical form. She lives in Abergavenny with her Jack Russell, Jasper, and spends her retirement writing, teaching small groups, and tending to the bountiful fruit trees, vegetables, and herbal plants that populate her magical organic garden.

For more information visit www.drblackwell.co.uk

www.ingramcontent.com/pod-product-compliance
Ingram Content Group UK Ltd.
Pitfield, Milton Keynes, MK11 3LW, UK
UKHW021853290625
6630UKWH00005B/383